The Welcome Back to School Book

by Jeri Carroll, Donna Beveridge, and Diane McCune

illustrated by Judy Hierstein

Cover by Judy Hierstein

Copyright © Good Apple, Inc., 1987

ISBN No. 0-86653-383-4

Printing No.

GOOD APPLE, INC.
BOX 299
CARTHAGE, IL 62321-0299

TABLE OF CONTENTS

INTRODUCTION

This book was written to serve as an aid to both beginning and experienced teachers as they begin a new year. Many student teachers have never begun a year with a fresh classroom, and many experienced teachers consult friends, colleagues, and idea books for new and challenging things to do in the room each year.

No matter how hard the teacher tries to make the beginning of each year run smoothly, there seems to be something that is forgotten and that is the one thing that is really needed—safety pins, scissors, glue, etc. THE FIRST PART OF THIS BOOK IS DESIGNED TO HELP TEACHERS SET UP THE ROOM BEFORE THE CHILDREN GET THERE. There are suggestions for welcoming students, preparing the teacher's desk, getting room decorations up, designing name tags for the children, putting up and using charts, arranging the students' desks, and having the classroom checklists ready for whatever may arise.

THE SECOND PART OF THE BOOK IS DESIGNED ESPECIALLY TO HELP WITH THAT FIRST DAY, FIRST WEEK, FIRST MONTH (page 38). There are activities to keep the children busy as you greet all the others, projects to get started that will continue throughout the year, motivating activities to get the children excited about getting back to the basics, games for learning about each other and reviewing skills, special units for use in the fall, guidelines for management, and aids that will support a positive parent involvement in your classroom.

LETTERS OF WELCOME

Dear _____,

I am glad that you are in my class this year. Many of you I know already. Others I will get to know very soon.

We have much to learn. I know that most of you are eager to learn to write in cursive, to practice multiplication facts, and to do science experiments. And think of all the good books we can read.

I hope this will be a special year for you. Please talk to me when you have something to share, when you don't understand, or when you are upset. I will try to listen very carefully. Will you be a good listener, too?

See you this week—and all year, too. Enjoy yourself!

Sincerely,

_____

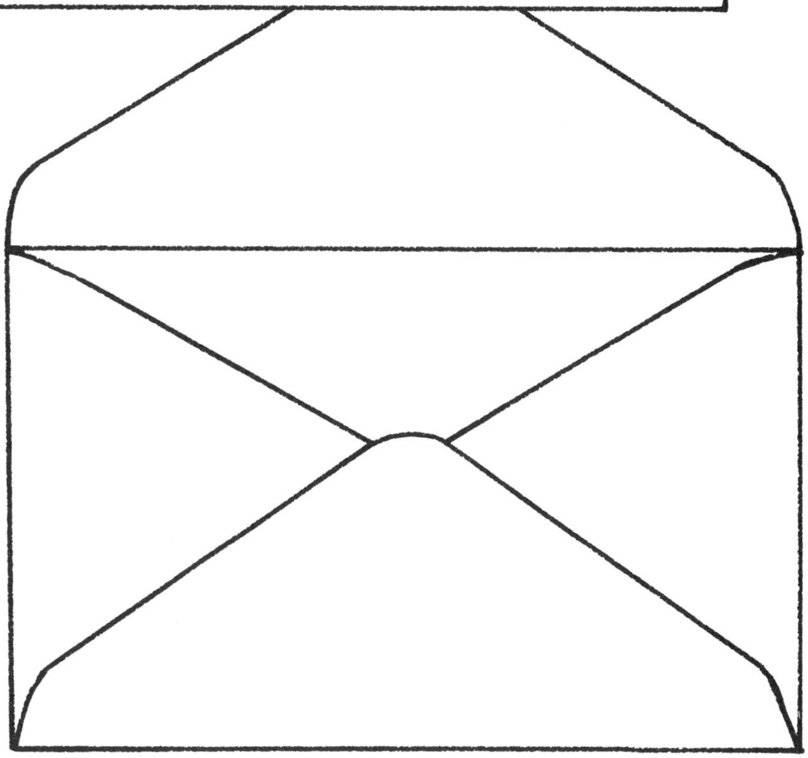

Dear _____,

I bet you are really excited about getting ready to come back to school. I am. I wonder who you are and you probably wonder who I am.

This year will be a fun one for us. We will be learning to read and playing with our friends. We will be learning to add and subtract and doing nice things for other people. We will study about ourselves and others, our town and other places. What a fun year!

Do you know what we will do the first day you are here? We will be playing some fun games to learn the names of all the other friends who will be here. I wonder if you will know everyone's name when you go home that first day.

I am looking forward to seeing you next week.

Sincerely,

_____

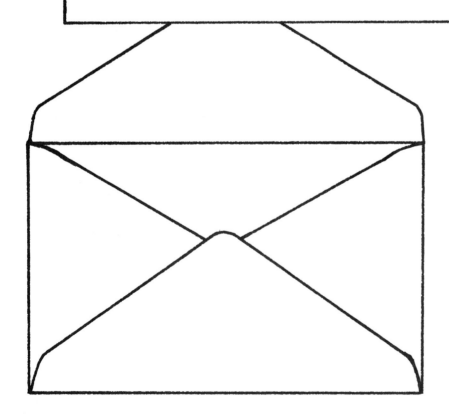

PREPARING THE DESK

ONE OF THE MOST INVALUABLE THINGS IN THE ROOM IS THE TEACHER'S DESK. There are several important items that can be stored in or near it that you should have with you during that first day and first week.

On the Desk

markers—all colors, broad tip, fine tip, permanent or watercolor

scissors—ones that actually cut things and extras for those who forget or never will have them. Be sure to include ones for those lefties.

bell or timer

stapler with staples

tape dispenser

rubber bands of various sizes and colors

paper clips—the standard ones from the office, large ones, colored ones and a magnet to hold a few on the desk for the children to use

pins—safety pins, straight pins, map marking pins, and tacks

pencils—colored, leaded, red for marking and extras to loan or sell to those who forget. Be sure to have a container of sharp pencils to loan to those who cannot find theirs or break a pencil during a lesson. To insure their return, have the child leave something in trade—a coat, sweater, shoe, etc. The pencil must be returned to get the article back.

erasers—have an assortment marked with identifying symbols, for the children to borrow. You might even tie a string around each eraser with a large object on the other end. It doesn't get lost as easily.

stamps and stamp pads—different stamps for praise

note paper, informal—to send notes to the teacher next door and to the students

formal—to send notes home to the parents

thank-you notes, informal—to send to the kids thanking them for their super help

formal—to send to those who help with the tasks of the room

glue, rubber cement

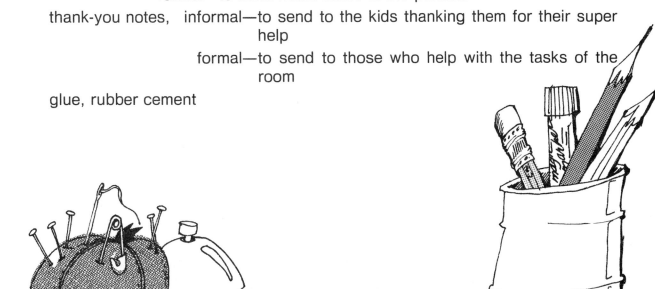

cards—birthday cards for the students and extras for faculty, cheer-up cards, get-well cards, etc.

reinforcer notes—to give to the children as they accomplish skills, have good days, lose teeth, avoid confrontations, etc.

file box—keep a card for each child with name, address, phone, and parents' names. Also keep one card for each child on which you can record noteworthy events—date them. These are useful for parent conferences, report cards, special education referrals, etc.

two books—one to read during a sustained silent reading period and one to read to the children

something personal from home—a photo of children, small piece of art, small terrarium, stuffed animal, etc. This makes you real to the children.

file system for loaning and borrowing of items

blindfold

vases of various sizes, narrow and wide-necked—pick them up at the garage and yard sales in the summer.

a whistle for outdoor games

a staff holder for chalk to make lines on the board for printing

letters for tracing, although it is better to learn to do it freehand to save time and energy.

Ticky Tack—a substitute for masking tape on walls. It can be used over and over.

stickers, rubber stamps, ink pads, reminders

tools—screwdriver, hammer, pliers, measuring tape, razor, X-acto knife. Keep on hand simple tools for easy repairs. It is good to have the children see you solve easy problems for yourself.

personal items—sewing kit, buttons, thread, needles, coffee cup, spoon, fork, plastic bowl and plastic plate, supply of instant coffee, teabags, sugar packets, bouillon and instant soups. A teacher's day is sometimes never done.

Check in the office for aspirin, Tums, Band-Aids, sanitary napkins, etc. Find the first aid box and know what is available in it. Check to see that it is current and full.

DOORS, BOARDS AND TAGS

Make your classroom special—choose a theme.

Choose a theme for the beginning of school. You can choose from the following or use one of your own.

Frogs:	Come in and Join Our Pad
Kids:	Be a Member of Our Patch
Hot Air Balloons:	Flying High in the Third Grade
Fashionable Children:	The ''In'' Crowd
Hip Fashions:	School Is Cool!
Wizard Hats:	Meet the Third Grade Wizards
Classified Ads:	Wanted: Fourth Graders
Pencils:	Sharp Students in Room 11
Rabbits in Hats:	Amazing Students
Mail:	First Class Students
Shapes:	New Shapes for a New Year
Parachutes:	Drop into Grade One
Apples (or other fruit):	The Pick of the Crop
Paint Splotches:	A Colorful Class
Footprints:	Grade Three: A Big Step
Runners:	Second Graders: On Your Mark
Clocks:	Time for First Grade

DOOR DECORATIONS

Decorate your door. Use the same theme and have a place where the children can put the name tags as they leave the room each day.

Have the children tape them onto the door as they leave, or decorate a pocket chart and have them place the name tags in the pockets.

FLYING HIGH IN THE THIRD GRADE

WELCOME TO OUR PAD

WANTED: THIRD GRADERS

tags go in large pocket

SHARP STUDENTS IN ROOM 11

tags slip into pencil
sharpener pocket

ENTRANCE: A YEAR OF MAGIC

rabbit tags go in hat

FIRST CLASS STUDENTS

3-D mailbox attached to door with
door that opens for tags

NEW SHAPES FOR 1987

individual pockets for shape tags

DROP INTO GRADE ONE

hooks on parachutes for parachute people tags

A COLORFUL CLASS

paint splotch tags taped to door

M-M-M-M-M-M-M
PICK OF THE CROP!

apple tags taped above basket

8

STEP UP AND STEP IN

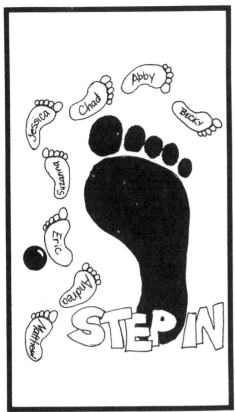

footprint tags taped to door

GO TO SECOND GRADE

T-shirt tags attach to runner

TIME FOR SCHOOL

clock tags taped to frame of door

BIG THINGS HAPPEN HERE

large animals with name on each

BULLETIN BOARDS FOR THE FIRST OF THE YEAR

Put up a bulletin board that has the children's names on it in some way. Follow the theme that you have chosen.

WANTED: THIRD GRADERS
Background: White or classified ads
Letters: Black

Names of students are written with a wide red marker on torn pieces of classified ads and mounted on black paper.

SCHOOL IS COOL!
Children select pictures of people dressed "cool" from *GQ*, *Seventeen*, and *Teen*. They put up these fashions for fall on the bulletin board with their names on them in some way.

SHARP STUDENTS IN 111
Background: Any strong color
Letters: Yellow
Yellow pencil for each child with name written in black or background color

AMAZING STUDENTS
Background: Yellow
Letters: Black
Rabbit in white for each child with name in black

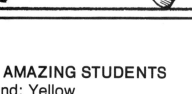

FIRST CLASS STUDENTS
Background: Blue
Mailbox: Silver
Flag: Red
Post: Brown
Envelope for each child

NEW SHAPES FOR A NEW YEAR
Background: Blue
Shapes: Yellow or multicolored
Letters and names: Blue or black
One shape for each child

DROP INTO GRADE ONE
Background: Blue
Clouds: White
Letters: Black or blue
Parachutes: Multicolored
Name on each chute in black

THE PICK OF THE CROP
Background: Blue
Trunk: Brown
Top of tree: Green
Basket: Brown
Apples

A COLORFUL CLASS
Background: White
Can: Silver with red lid
Splotches: Multicolored
Brush: Brown with red paint

GRADE 3: A BIG STEP
Background: Yellow
Footprints: Black
Letters: Yellow
Names written on yellow paper glued to feet

SECOND GRADERS: ON YOUR MARK
Background: Green
Line: Black
Runners: Multicolored with white name card on each
Letters: Black or colored

TIME FOR FIRST GRADE
Background: White
Large clock or watch: Red frame, white face, black hands, and numbers
Letters: Red

COME IN AND JOIN OUR PAD
Water: Brown or blue
Pads: Green
One frog per child with name in black

BE A MEMBER OF OUR PATCH
Background: Blue
Leaves: Green
Children make pictures of faces and choose leaf on board. Name goes on leaf.

FLY HIGH IN GRADE THREE
Background: Blue
Baskets: Brown with child's name
Balloons: White
Child decorates balloon

THE ''IN'' CROWD
Children draw pictures of themselves to put on board. Names go below each child.

NAME TAGS

Make name tags for the children to wear those first few days. Have them match the bulletin board designs. It is sometimes best to cut out the patterns ahead of time. Let the child tell you what he or she wants to be called and then put the name on the card.

Make sure you are flexible. You probably will not have all the children on your list and have some you have never heard of. You will probably have a few who belong in another room and will only discover that at lunch. And there are always those who don't enter until the second or third day of school. In order to make each child feel comfortable even though you do not have him on your list, keep pins, magic markers, Con-Tact paper, and extras of everything handy for that first day.

RABBIT PATTERN

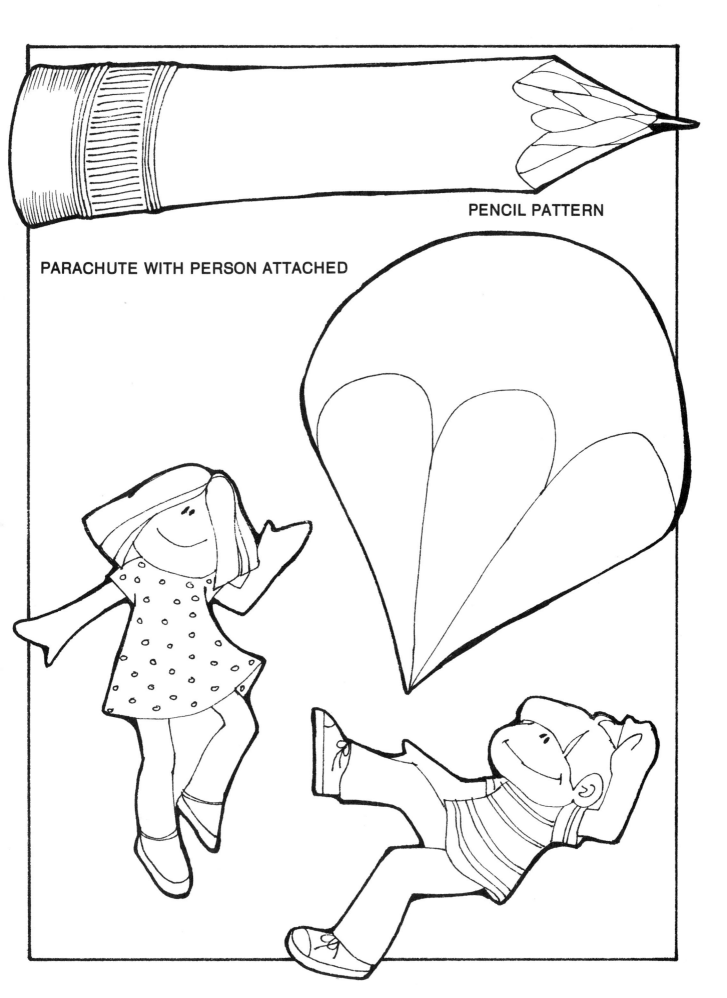

PENCIL PATTERN

PARACHUTE WITH PERSON ATTACHED

15

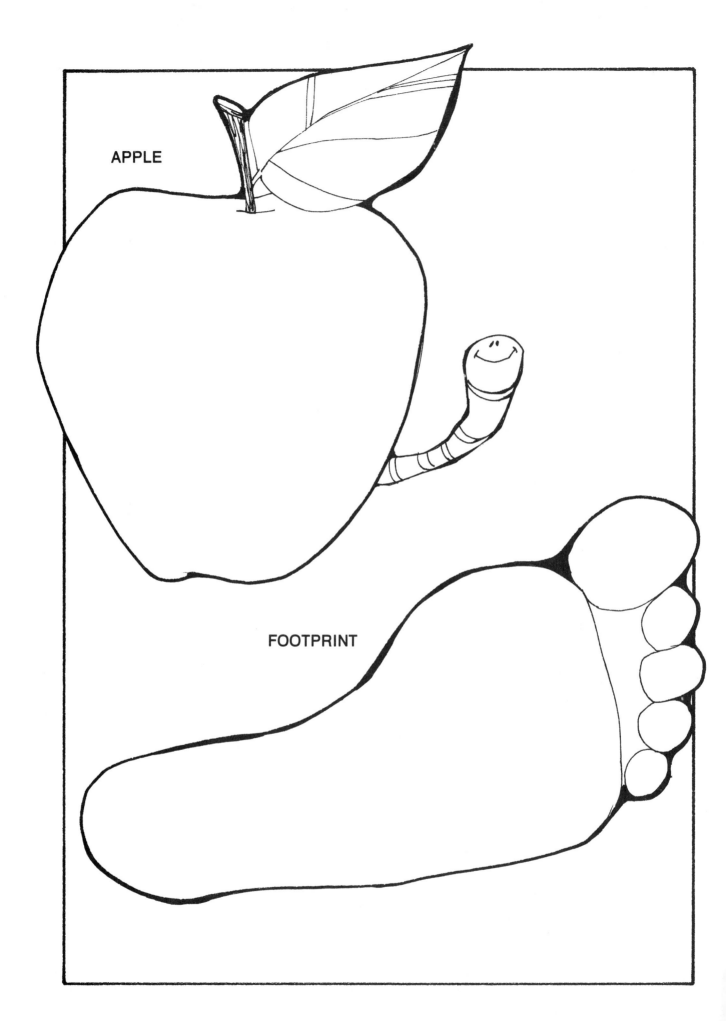

APPLE

FOOTPRINT

16

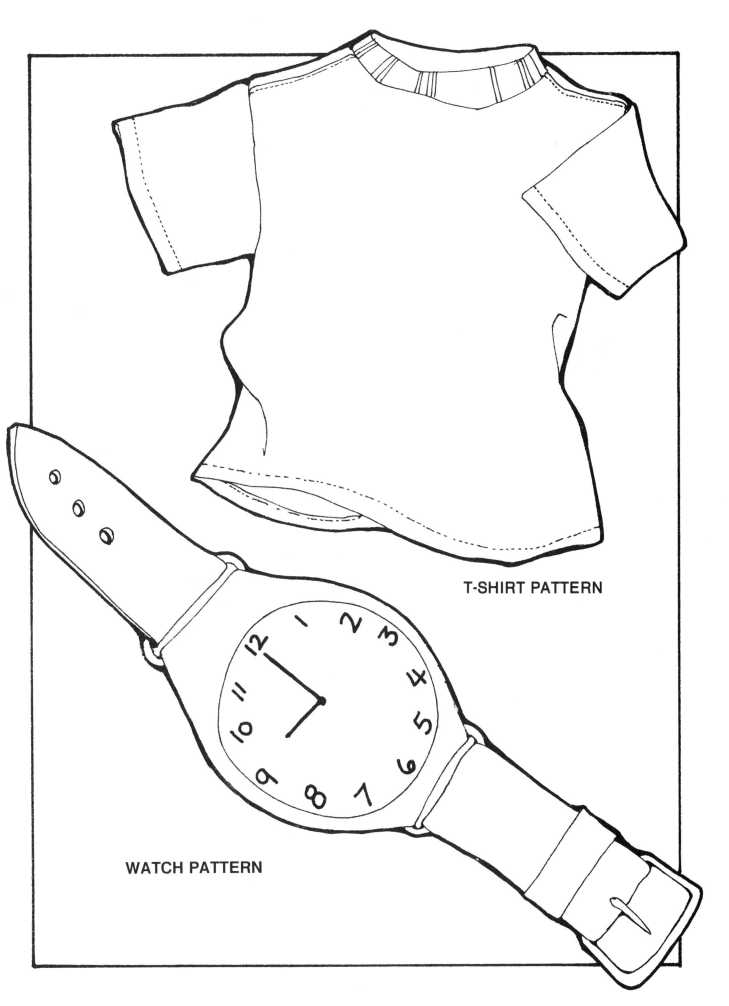

T-SHIRT PATTERN

WATCH PATTERN

17

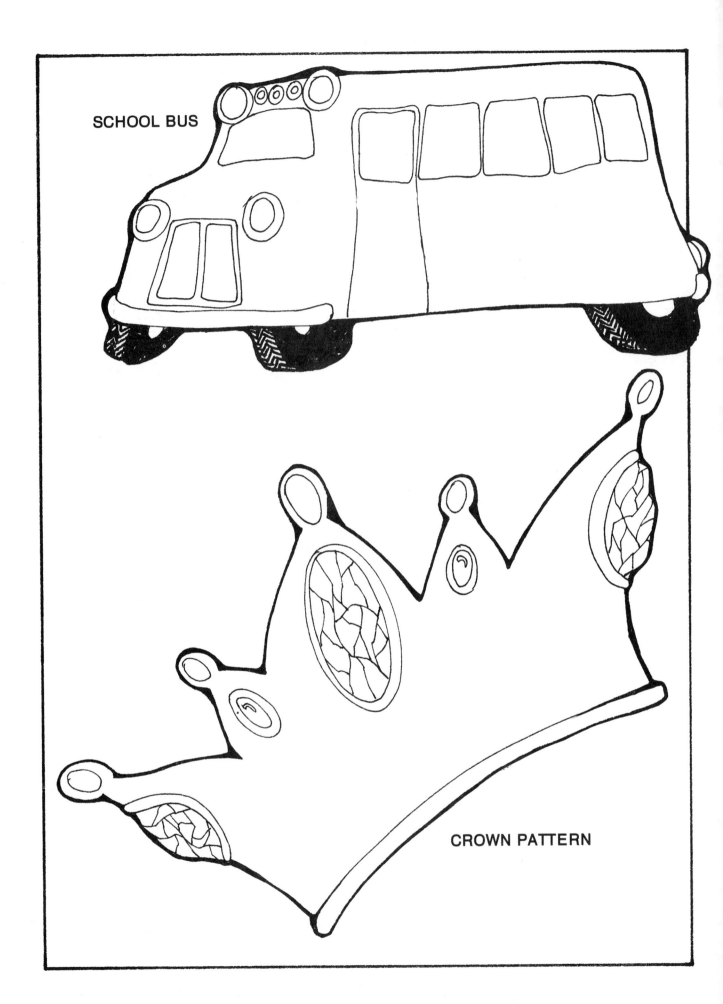

SCHOOL BUS

CROWN PATTERN

CHARTS

HELPER

Children need to have responsibilities in order to become responsible adults.

All helper charts should be attractively titled. The teacher should provide a set of markers which have the child's name on them to match the chart. The chart should have tasks in written or picture form—or both—depending on the age of the group so that the children can tell from reading the chart just what they are to do. Remember to keep the jobs important. Let the children have some say in the jobs that are listed or in what they want to do.

There are many tasks that they can perform in the classroom:

lead line	end line
feed animals	water plants
check coat room	monitor playground equipment
empty trash	run errands
hold flag	lead flag salute
pass out snacks/milk	read helper chart
change calendar	pass out materials/supplies
lead the reading	check row for trash
pass out notes to be taken home	hand back papers (ungraded ones,
clean the tables	only)

Job Titles Can Be Fun
Zookeeper—feeds the animals
T.A.—Teacher Assistant—any job not covered by other jobs
U.P.S.—United Person Service (does errands outside the classroom)
Lunch Spy—watches to see when it is our turn for lunch
Chalker—claps erasers, writes date on board each day
Janitor—keeps floor and closet clean
Mailer—puts corrected papers and notices into cubbies

Keep records of children's job choices, and let everyone have a turn at a job before others get seconds.

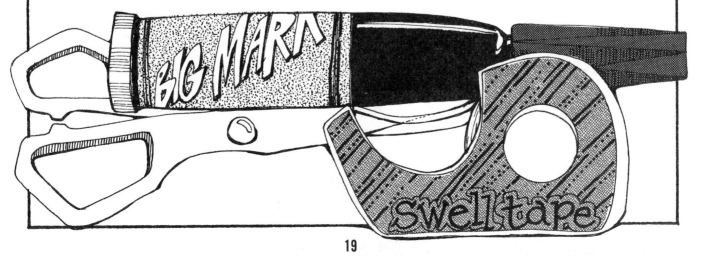

There are many themes to these charts and many ways to present them.

Don't Just Stand There—Help!

Each child traces his foot, decorates it, and puts his name on it. On the bulletin board are several tasks listed on a chart. The feet are standing nearby to be placed on the chart. Or the feet are attached to the board in random order. Each foot has a job listed on it. Library packets hold 3'' x 5'' cards with names of all the children who are to have the jobs.

Busy Hands

Each child traces his own hand and puts his name on it. The hands are placed on the bulletin board at varying distances. The tasks for the room are on construction paper handprints. The handprints are joined with a string or moved to match.

Busy as Beavers

Around a large beaver are chewed pieces of wood with class jobs written on each. The child's name is placed on one of these pieces of wood to show the task to be done. A small beaver name tag can be used and attached to each piece of wood to show who is doing the job.

Working Hand in Hand
Paper doll cutouts joined hand in hand are attached to the wall in a circle. A student's name is written on each cutout doll. File card names indicate what each student's job is.

Job Wheel
A large and a small circle of contrasting colors are joined in the center with a paper brad. The inner circle contains the jobs. The outer circle contains the names of all the children. There should be half as many jobs as students. When it is time to change jobs, the inner wheel is moved one job to the right. A child gets a job every other job change. This is especially good for the younger children who can't wait very long.

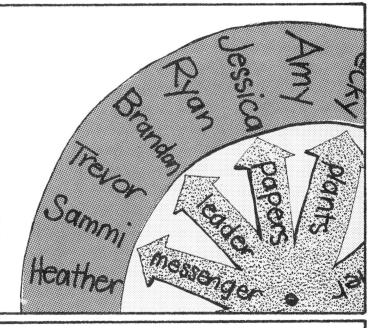

Busy Bees
Let the children make the background for the chart by providing each with a piece of paper to make part of the honeycomb. Each part of the comb will have a job labeled on it. Put that up as the background. Each child can make a bee and put his name on it. The bees are placed on the appropriate jobs.

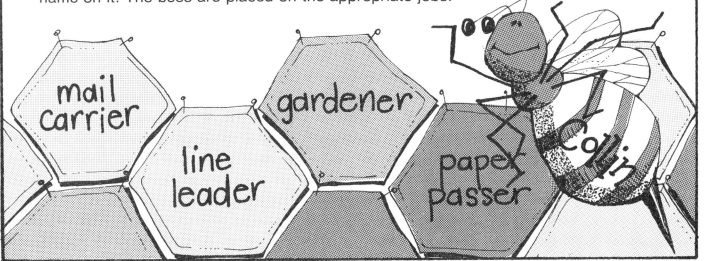

BIRTHDAY

Celebrate the birthday of every child, even those with summer and holiday birthdays. Have "nonbirthdays" or "unbirthdays" for them at a surprise time during the year.

Make a birthday chart for the year. Include your own birthday and the birthdays of other people important to the children.

Ways to celebrate:

Join the lunch bunch—invite parents or adult friends to lunch.

Sing "Happy Birthday" or "It's a Very Merry Unbirthday for You."

Make cards for the birthday person.

Make a crown for the person's head, a sash, or a felt chair cover for the back of his chair.

Be "first" all day.

Choose any class job for the day.

Receive a birthday telegram from the principal.

Choose a record to listen to during the last five minutes before lunch.

Names on fruit, names on balloons, names on cupcakes

Birthdays Are Special

Would you like to help celebrate your child's birthday by coming for lunch on _____? Please bring your own lunch. You may bring a treat for the class, but it is not necessary. Come at _____. If you cannot come, perhaps a grandparent or adult friend can join us. Young children at home are welcome.

Special Invitation

You are cordially invited to visit

_____

class on _____ at _____.
We would appreciate your sharing
information about _____
_____ when you come.
Thank you,

Place a chart on the bulletin board that lists the nine or ten months that your children attend school.

Each time a child loses a tooth, he records the date and name on a white tooth and places it in the appropriate slot.

A tooth lost at school can be gold instead of white.

At the end of the year, graph the number of teeth lost each month to see when the most teeth were lost.

Ask questions about the graph.
How many teeth were lost each month?
How many teeth were lost at school each month?
How many teeth were lost in September?
Who lost the most teeth?

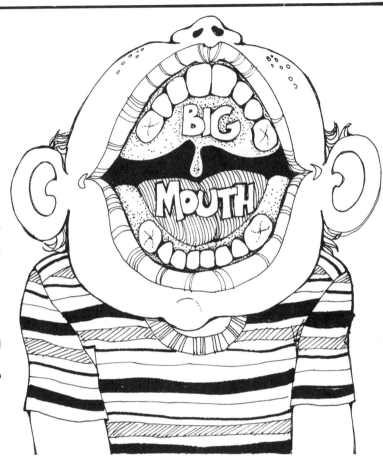

TOOTH GRAPH

T O O T H G R A P H	Sally							
	Central Incisors	Central Incisors	Lateral Incisors	Lateral Incisors	Cuspids (pointed)	Cuspids (pointed)	Pre-molars	Pre-molars
	Upper 2 front	Lower 2 front	Upper	Lower	Upper	Lower	Upper	Lower

Place cutout teeth on graph. Put name on tooth.

CALENDARS

Calendars are important to any elementary classroom. The children are just beginning to learn about time and understand the past, present, and future. The calendar helps with this as does the use of time lines (see Time Lines).

Many types of calendars are available for purchase, but one that is best suited for your use is the one that you make. Take a large piece of poster board and make a blank calendar, putting in the names of the days of the week. Do not put the month on it and be sure to allow at least five rows for weeks. Some months will use six rows, but the use of five for classrooms is probably good enough. Laminate the calendar before you begin using it.

Staple strips of colored paper to the bulletin board to make a calendar outline. The first week can be red, the second yellow, the third green, the fourth pink, the fifth blue. Make lines down the strips to make the days.

Place a manila envelope near the calendar and fill it with symbols appropriate for the month (apples for September, etc.). Fill in the calendar day by day with symbols appropriate to the month made by the children or use the patterns provided here. At the end of the month the symbols can go in a train car named for the month. The train grows as the school year passes.

Place the name of the month at the top of a bulletin board. Put five rows of seven library pockets in the configuration of a calendar. Write the name of the day on the pocket. Nearby have a set of 3'' x 5'' cards that have numbers on them. When it is the first of the month, place the one in the appropriate pocket. Special events can be recorded by special pictures (a firecracker for the 4th of July) or a child's name (Molly's birthday) on these 3'' x 5'' cards. At the end of the month the only thing that needs to be done is to pull the numbers from the pockets and change the name at the top of the calendar.

Use permanent magic marker to write the name of the month on the calendar in the spot that you left for it. (You can wipe this off the laminated poster board at the end of the month with cheap hair spray.)

Number the days in the same way.

Cut out the appropriate number of patterns for each day of the month and put a number on each.

Place the numbers for the calendar in an envelope and post it near the calendar.

As part of the opening each day, have the children put up the number for the day of the week and say the appropriate sentence to label the day, month, date, and year. ''Today is Wednesday, December 4, 1987.''

Keep the permanent magic marker close at hand. Record any important events on the calendar with the magic marker.

Most of us use calendars with the children, but use only one calendar. Try using separate calendars for each month and saving them. Take a look at the months past on the first of each month as you change calendars. If you have two classes, one in the a.m. and one in the p.m., use one side of the calendar for the morning group and one for the afternoon group. Record various types of events on the calendars: weather, birthdays, holidays, vacation days, field trips, unit topics, people visiting, etc.

If you want to get a little bit more technical, use actual calendars of the months to represent the months rather than pieces of construction paper. The calendars could be put up linearly to represent the year. Children can talk about things that have happened in the past, what they have done in the past few days, are doing today and will be doing tomorrow, and can look forward to the approaching events that are in the "distant" future. Time comes alive.

APRIL

Sunday	Monday	Tuesday	Wednesday	Thursday	Friday	Saturday
	1	2	3	4	5	6
7	8 ann has a brother	9	10	11	12	13
14	15	16	17	18	19 HOSPITAL Field Trip	20
21	22	23	24	25	26	27
28	29	30	31	MAY is COMING		

BLANK CALENDAR

Sunday	Monday	Tuesday	Wednesday	Thursday	Friday	Saturday

CALENDAR PATTERNS

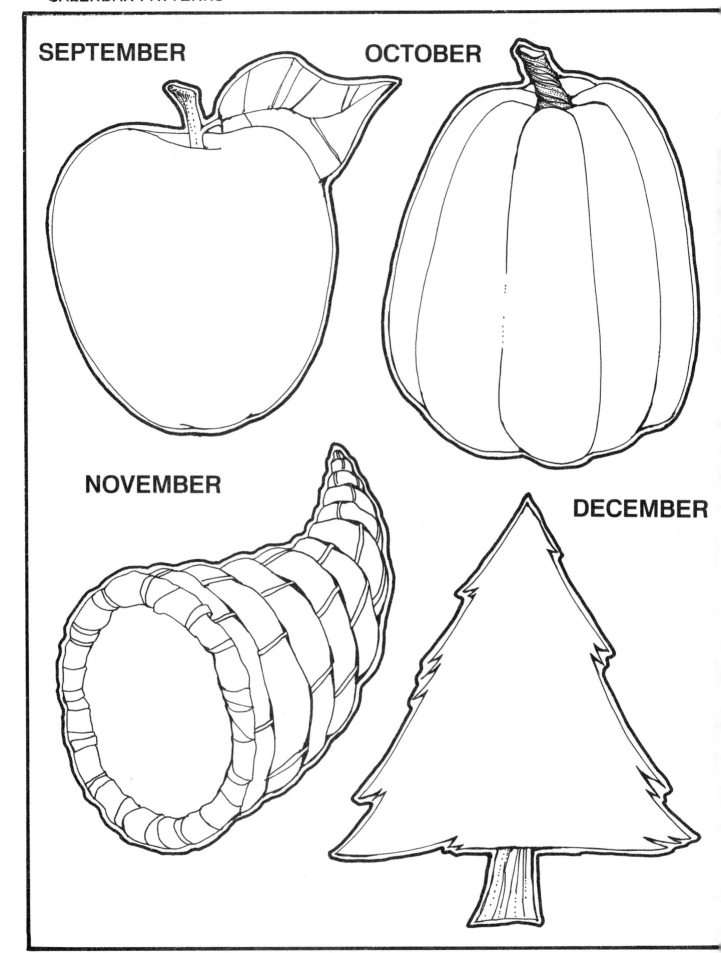

SEPTEMBER

OCTOBER

NOVEMBER

DECEMBER

JANUARY

FEBRUARY

MARCH

APRIL

MAY

JUNE

JULY

AUGUST

TIME LINES

In order for children to understand more accurately the time element in history, time lines can be invaluable. For the very young children, a record of the happenings can suffice. For the older children, records of what they are studying in history, geography, health, art, music, etc., can show when things happened.

Try any one of the following methods of time lines for your group.

Copy the master calendar kept each month with important events noted. The master calendar is probably on large poster board on the bulletin board. The copy can be on ditto-sized paper. Place the copy of the month's activities on a piece of 8'' x 12'' construction paper and use a different color for each month. Post these in the room.

Attach butcher paper to the walls of the room about six inches from the ceiling. Mark off large sections into centuries. As the children study about different people, places, events, inventions, etc., have them place symbols in the appropriate centuries.

Attach butcher paper to the walls of the room where the children can get to it. Mark off large sections into decades. Have the children interview family members and find out their birth dates. Record those on the time line and put up pictures of the persons. Children can put up their own pictures at the appropriate places.

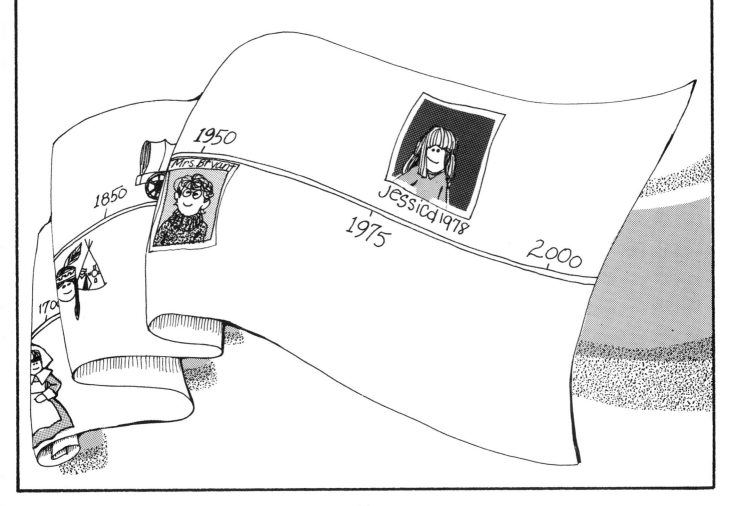

Monthly Calendars

Use a time line in your room. This time line should be very concrete for beginners. Put up a piece of construction paper for the month when you begin the year. It can be 9'' x 12'' or 12'' x 18''. Label the piece of paper at the bottom with the name of the month and use a color that is appropriate for that time of the year. As the month passes, place pictures on the piece of construction paper that show important events that happened in the life of your class. For instance, September might have pictures of your school, your class, an apple (to show a unit of Johnny Appleseed), a birthday cake with Callie's name on it (to show that Callie's birthday is in September), etc.

SEPTEMBER   OCTOBER   NOVEMBER   DECEMBER

Each month add a piece of construction paper to show the coming of another month. If your children can handle it, put enough sheets of paper up at the beginning to show the entire year. You can put events that are going to happen in the future on the appropiate places.

Time Lines for Teaching History

As we talk with children about events in the past, it helps them put them into perspective if they can see a picture of when these things happened. We all tend to discuss the Pilgrims and Indians when we talk about Thanksgiving. We talk about Christopher Columbus on Columbus Day. We tell children about George Washington and Abraham Lincoln in February. We talk about Martin Luther King, Jr., in January. As far as children are concerned, these people could all be alive or could have recently died or could be cartoon people. We need to help them *see* when these people lived.

Put up large sections of paper—one yard by four yards—to represent centuries. Most things we discuss with young children in the United States begin around 1500—Columbus was 1492. You can have one for the 1500's, one for the 1600's, one for the 1700's, one for the 1800's, and one for the 1900's.

As you read about people such as Columbus, Washington, Lincoln, King or events (Independence Day, the state's birthday, holidays, birthdays), place symbols on the appropriate centuries to let the children *see* when these people lived or when these events happened. Children can bring in pictures of themselves as babies, their parents as babies, their grandparents, etc., to show when they were born.

ROOM ARRANGEMENTS

Take a good look at your room. Have you been there before? Are you getting tired of the same old stuff? Is it a new place for you? What are you going to do with it?

Make It Work for You
Keep all dividers low to avoid blind spots where children can hide from you and do whatever they want.
Provide open spots for physical activity.
Provide quiet spots for reading, group discussions, and solitude.
Provide areas for center activities.
Make a stage. Two sets of porch steps covered with carpet make a special place to read, act, present, etc. Under the stairs is great for storage.

Storage Hints
Use the dividers for storage.
Use unit boxes for storage of unit materials. Decorate them and use them for dividers.
Minimize the space for the teacher's desk. You won't spend much time sitting there anyway.
Store your materials at school. If you take them home, they will never be there when you need them.
Save only what is good, and save only a sample of that.
Organize your materials. Do one subject at a time, but get it done.
Label everything. That way everyone can help keep things organized.

Make It Safe
Avoid the use of extension cords.
Watch that those old carpets aren't shaggy—tape them to the floor.
Don't have those old tables with sharp corners where the kids can fall against them.
Don't set up places where children can avoid your sight.

Make It Work for Children
Make cubbies for their papers. Wooden ones are great, but you can use beverage boxes, ice-cream cartons, or large vegetable cans stacked on their sides. Avoid rolling by bolting them to a board.
Make sure children have adequate space for their coats, etc.
Teach them how to organize a desk.

Suggested Room Arrangements

You might think that the way you have your desks is the best for you and your room. If you haven't changed in the last month, you might not know that. Each group of children will react differently, and you will change from year to year.

There are several things to keep in mind when arranging the room.

Arrange desks so that all of the children can see you or the board without turning their chairs.

Have easy access for working with individuals. Don't use closed rectangles.

If space is a consideration, avoid rows.

Provide for ease in working in groups.

Make the best use of the natural light.

Minimize distractions from windows and doors.

The teacher's desk does not need to face the children.

Keep the space in front of children's desks free for activities and ease of teaching.

Consider having no desks. Use tables instead.

Common Desk Arrangements

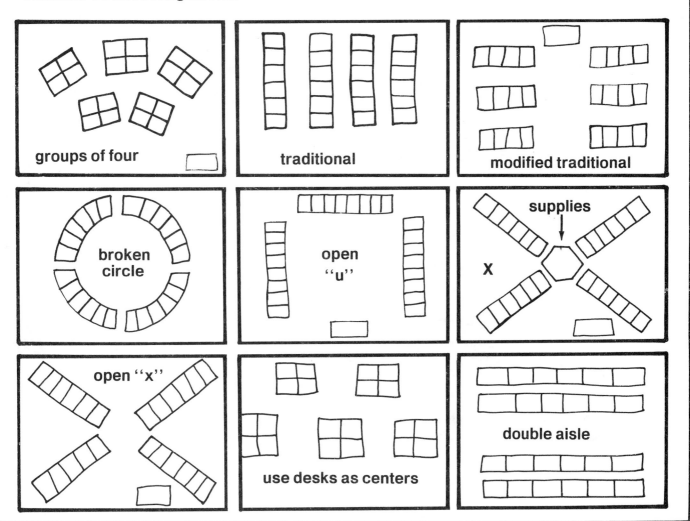

groups of four

traditional

modified traditional

broken circle

open "u"

X · supplies

open "x"

use desks as centers

double aisle

35

CLASS CHECKLISTS

On the following page is a blank checklist that you can use year after year for your class. There are six columns across the page plus one on the far left for your students' names.

Xerox one copy of the Class Checklist from this book before you attempt to use it. After you have copied it, alphabetize your students' names by first name and place them on the copied Class Checklist. Run several copies of this Class Checklist and keep them on your desk. You will find several uses for the six columns across the page.

First Week:
　　fees paid
　　information card returned
　　registration papers filed
　　physical forms in
　　dental cards
　　lunch money paid

　　name of student child played with
　　name of student child sat by voluntarily
　　name of student chosen as best friend
　　name of student child avoids
　　name of student who avoids the child

check if you have
　　called on the child to share a summer experience
　　called on the child to read from the assignment
　　called on the child to be the leader
　　written a positive note home to the parents
　　given the child a positive stroke for the day

Post the Class Checklist beside the helper chart and write the task that each child performs each week in order to keep track of who has done what.

Post the Class Checklist in the learning center and have the children check off when they have been in the center.

Put a Class Checklist in each of the "in baskets" in the room. Each time a child hands in a paper, have him check off the name on the list. This offers you a quick check to see who has done what during the day.

Use Class Checklists as interview sheets. Give one to each child and have the children interview every other child in the class, asking each child six questions and then seeing which children made similar choices.

Name							

THE KIDS ARE HERE! NOW WHAT?
CAMERA CAPERS

There are so many things that you can do with a camera that you should try to have one just for your room. It is an expense, but you can get one at a garage sale, or as a free gift if you subscribe to some magazines.

Take pictures of the children the first day and have the roll developed with two copies of each picture. Use them for a bulletin board, helper chart, labelling coat racks, door decorations, or gifts to send home to the parents.

Get a map of the community and place the pictures of the children where they live on the map.

Me and My Family
Paste the picture of the child on a piece of paper and have him draw the other members of his family.

Place a class list on your classroom door and put the children's pictures next to their names.

Take pictures of other important people in the building and in the main office of the school system. Label the pictures with names and jobs. Use this as a getting-to-know-the-system activity as well as a language arts activity for vocabulary building. It is great when the kindergartner can say, "I know you, Dr. Knox. You are the superintendent."

Use a close-up photo of each child's face as the basis for a paper doll. Let the children trace around a doll pattern and glue their faces on. They can then make clothes to fit the season, the unit, the times.

WANTED BY THE FBI: A FANTASTIC BUNCH OF INDIVIDUALS

Take pictures of the children on the first Monday of each month. Send the pictures home to the parents at the end of the year or to the mothers on Mother's Day.

Take pictures of a favorite tree nearby on the first Monday of each month. Post the pictures and talk about the changes.

Take pictures from one spot facing one direction at the same time of day on the first Monday of each month. Notice the changes.

Take slides all year long and show them to the parents and children on the last day of school.

LEARN ABOUT THE CHILDREN

Tell a Tale About Yourself
Unwind a small ball of yarn as you spin a yarn about yourself. Talk until the ball is all unwound. The next person winds the yarn into a ball while ''spinning the yarn.'' Check that each person gets a turn over a certain period of time before you go around the class a second time.

Ball Toss
Using a Nerf ball or some other type of lightweight ball, toss the ball to a person who has to tell something of interest about himself. He tosses it to another person until each child gets a chance.

Sign in on Chalkboard
As the teacher, sign your name and draw a picture of something you like very much or do well. Indicate what name you like to be called. As the children arrive, they can find a blank spot at the chalkboard and do the same. If it is too confusing, rotate them to the chalkboard throughout the day. Be sure to save this for several days. Use colored chalk the second day so children can color and decorate their drawings.

Go to the Head of the Class
Get to know one another by classifying and reclassifying children on the basis of likes, dislikes, families, physical attributes, etc.

1. Give the attributes and let the children classify themselves.
2. Group the children and have them determine what they have in common.
3. Let the children take turns classifying themselves.

Examples: Go to the head of the class if you . . .

have brown eyes
have braces
have a pet larger than a bread box
play sports on a team
love stuffed animals
eat raw vegetables
had breakfast this morning
have a brother or sister
have ever gone to another school
were nervous on the first day of school
went to the library more than three times this summer
carried a backpack to school today
have a hearty laugh
like to hug or be hugged
are wearing sneakers
know the name of our principal
have a sharp pencil

THE FIRST DAY

THAT FIRST HOUR

That first day of school is always so filled with administrative duties that we wonder what we will get done and how we can get the children motivated to return the next day. There are a few things the children can do that will free you to do what you need to do.

Select and read or look at a book.

Read letters written by last year's class at the end of the year, making sure that there is one letter for each child.

Draw and color pieces for a mural.

Give children bags of goodies to play with. Tell them after about five minutes that they can join with another or exchange baggies. Baggies can contain:

crayons and paper	Legos
watercolors and paper	beads and string
markers and paper	pegs and pegboards
colored pencils and paper	sewing cards
electronic game	book
book and tape	Lotto
board and grease pencil	magic slate
finger puppets	note cards and pen

Let children quietly explore the room and the centers. They may wish to write or draw in a journal that you have provided.

Create name tags.

Make collages of all the things that they like or did this summer.

Fill out Interest Inventories.

Make lists of favorite books.

Guess how many marbles are in a set of jars.

Choose desks and chairs that fit.

Work on activity sheets found on the desks.

Sign in on the sign-in sheet, bulletin board, or chalkboard.

Find pencil sharpener and sharpen one pencil.

Find the coat hooks in the classroom and mark with their names.

Find messages that have been placed in their mailboxes.

My name is Troy

I like the color red.

CHILDREN LEARN ABOUT SCHOOL

School/Classroom Trivia

Draw an outline of a bus for each team on the chalkboard. Put a number in each window. When a child answers a question correctly, he colors in the window. The first team to fill in all the windows is the winner. Each number corresponds to a particular question. Each team has its own set of questions.

Examples of Questions That Might Be Asked:
1. What is the name of the principal?
2. What is your teacher's first name?
3. What is the name of the school?
4. Who is your bus driver?
5. Where do we go during a fire drill?
6. Where is the library?
7. What time does school begin?
8. How much does hot lunch cost?
9. What time should you come to school?
10. Who are the other second grade teachers?
11. What days do we have art and music?
12. What's on the bulletin board in our hallway?

School Tour

Read the book, *The Gingerbread Boy,* up to the part where he is on the back of the fox. Ask the children if they know what is going to happen next. Ask if they want to save him from the fox. Then follow the Gingerbread Trail (paper gingerbread cutouts that are taped to the floor or wall and lead to prearranged school personnel—nurse, cook, custodian, librarian, etc., ending with the principal). At each stop the children ask for help in saving the Gingerbread Boy from the fox. The person explains how he has been too busy working and hasn't seen any gingerbread people and goes on to introduce himself and tell about his school job. The children can ask questions before following the trail to the next person. At the last stop after the children ask the principal for help, the principal says the best way to keep the Gingerbread Boy out of the mouth of the fox is for the children to eat him first. A box or tray of cookies is produced—or the principal leads them to the kitchen—and the children take them to their room for snack time and the ending of the story.

FIRST DAY ACTIVITIES

A New Word
Teach a word that will sound impressive, be useful, or both. Let children enjoy showing off to parents and brothers and sisters. *Sesquipedalian* is a good one to use—it is a use of long words. Children love to say and use it. Better yet—most families don't know the word.

Something About the Teacher and Each Classmate
Get acquainted. Play name games. Share about yourselves in pictures or in words. Let your children know that you are not only a teacher, but that you are a parent, child, student, athlete, etc.; that you have a first name, special likes and dislikes, problems, dreams, favored foods, and dislike chores; that you live in a community just as they do.

Class and School Rules
Rules should be written and a copy sent home for each child. Be sure to go over playground rules before the first recess. School and class rules need to be kept simple with expectations that they will be and can be followed.

Listening to a Story
Build enthusiasm for reading correctly from day one. Make sure that every day includes story time. Children will often enjoy stories that they are not yet able to read independently. Gather the children around you. Sit on the floor or in a rocker. Don't be afraid to throw yourself into the story by using character voices or actions. Children love listening to a reader who makes a story come alive.

Writing
The excitement is there as well for writing as reading. The children have new sharp pencils and fresh white paper. Have them write something—tell about themselves, apply for class jobs, write in their journals, write about their summer, write their names in their journals, list questions that they have about their new grade, copy names of classmates, write about their first day of school.

Receiving New Books
Even if texts or workbooks are infrequently used, it is special to children to be able to handle books for their new grade, to thumb through them to see what they might be going to learn, and to be able to place them carefully in a desk that will rarely be neat again all year.

Creating a "Take-Home Product"
Children want something to share with their families, something that they "made at school today"—a drawing, collage, model, a fun paper, freebies from the teacher, etc.

Interacting with the Classroom/School Environment
Give them the chance to explore the playground boundaries, use the equipment, learn their way from one place to another, look at and touch things in the room, get to know where the bathrooms and water fountains are.

DARE TO BE DIFFERENT

Try this one. Don't decorate or arrange the room for the first day of school. Let the children make the room their own.

Discuss classroom needs, and let the children arrange open spaces, work spaces, desk arrangement.

Have a set of supplies on hand—paper, scissors, decorations, paint, letters to trace, etc.,—and let them decorate the room with individual or group artwork.

Let them make lists of suggested topics for studying during the year.

Have them develop curiosity questions for which they would like to find answers.

Arrange child materials for easy access.

Let them choose their own closet hooks, cubbies, and mailboxes and make labels for each so that they belong to them.

Discuss what could be done to make school a better place for everyone.

Read the poem "If I Ran the School" by Betsy Swyers in *Teacher,* September, 1974. It will generate ideas for making the school a great place.

See How I Grow

Measure each child's height. Write the name and date and display where children can measure themselves during the year. Record weights, too, if it isn't too touchy.

Guess How Many

Estimate the number of marbles in a jar, children in the school, kids in the class, visitors at Open House, blocks in the box, candies in a bag.

1. Let everyone guess. Provide no clues. List everyone's guess on overhead, chalkboard, or chart paper. Discuss guesses. Whose guess is greatest? Whose guess is one less than Dave's?
2. Provide some information to help children make a better guess or "guesstimate." Remove all marbles of one color and count. Children then make a "guesstimate" based on limited information. They may keep their first guess or change it. Again list their choices. Discuss. Whose "guesstimate" is higher than their guess? Whose is lower? Who chose an even number?
3. Provide further information to help the children make an informed guess, an "estimate." Again, have the children "estimate" and record their choices. Discuss. What's the difference between the highest and lowest choices?
4. Count.

WARM FUZZIES (WE ALL NEED THEM)

Phone-a-Great Calls
Teachers call parents when there are problems. How about calling each parent as soon as possible once the year begins for no other reason than to say something great about each child. (There is something special about everyone.) This starts the year off on a positive note. Continue this policy throughout the year. The children love it.

Sunshine Grams
During the first week be sure that each child receives a Sunshine Gram. You brightened my day by . . . .

The Sunshine Grams may be written by you or by the children for each other. As children get older, the ones from their peers mean more than the ones from the teacher.

Continue this process throughout the year. There are many reproducibles available to provide variety.

Hug-Ins
Put up a sign on the wall:
HAVE YOU HUGGED YOUR TEACHER TODAY?
or
I'M A HUGGER. ARE YOU?

Whoever wishes may come for a hug from you or hug each other. It does wonders on those days that are slow starters for everyone.

Our Class Tree
Students cut leaf designs out of very thin screen. The leaves are sprayed orange, yellow, red and added to a large empty branch in the room. In the center of the leaf, the child puts an individual picture of himself.

INVENTORIES

Interest Inventories
These will help you find out about your children: what they like, what they don't like, what they know, how they learn, who they are, etc.

Use the information that you collect to
   put the children into learning groups
   select members for physical education teams
   seat children in the room
   develop learning centers
   decide what games to make and purchase

Textbook Reviews
Have the children spend some time examining the books that they will be using for the year. Upper grade children can fill out a textbook review form.
Younger children can
   draw pictures of the things they find interesting
   write captions to interesting pictures
   copy the table of contents

Use the information from these textbook examinations
to decide
   which units will need in-depth study
   which have already been covered
   which are of interest to the children
   which you can make self-teaching materials for

From this information you can make up a list of topics for the librarian. She can then pull books on that topic to use during the time you will be studying the topic.

Make up notes to send home to parents requesting their expertise during the study of certain topics which are of particular interest to their children.

INTEREST INVENTORY

Grade _____

Name _____

Date _____

1. If you cannot watch television at home, what would you most like to do? _____

   _____

   _____

   _____

   _____

2. If your parents told you that you could do anything that you wanted to do this

   weekend, what would you choose? _____

   _____

   _____

   _____

3. What is your favorite subject in school? _____

4. What subject is most difficult for you in school? _____

5. If you could learn about anything you wanted to learn about, what would you

   choose? _____

   _____

   _____

6. What is your favorite television show? _____

_____

7. What book or story have you read recently that was really exciting for you? __

_____

_____

8. What is the most fun thing to do inside besides watching television? _____

_____

9. Do you like to do your work best in groups or alone? _____

_____

_____

10. Do you do your best work in groups or when you work alone? _____

_____

11. Would you rather read a book or watch a movie if you have to learn something?

_____

_____

_____

12. Who are your two best friends in this class? _____

_____

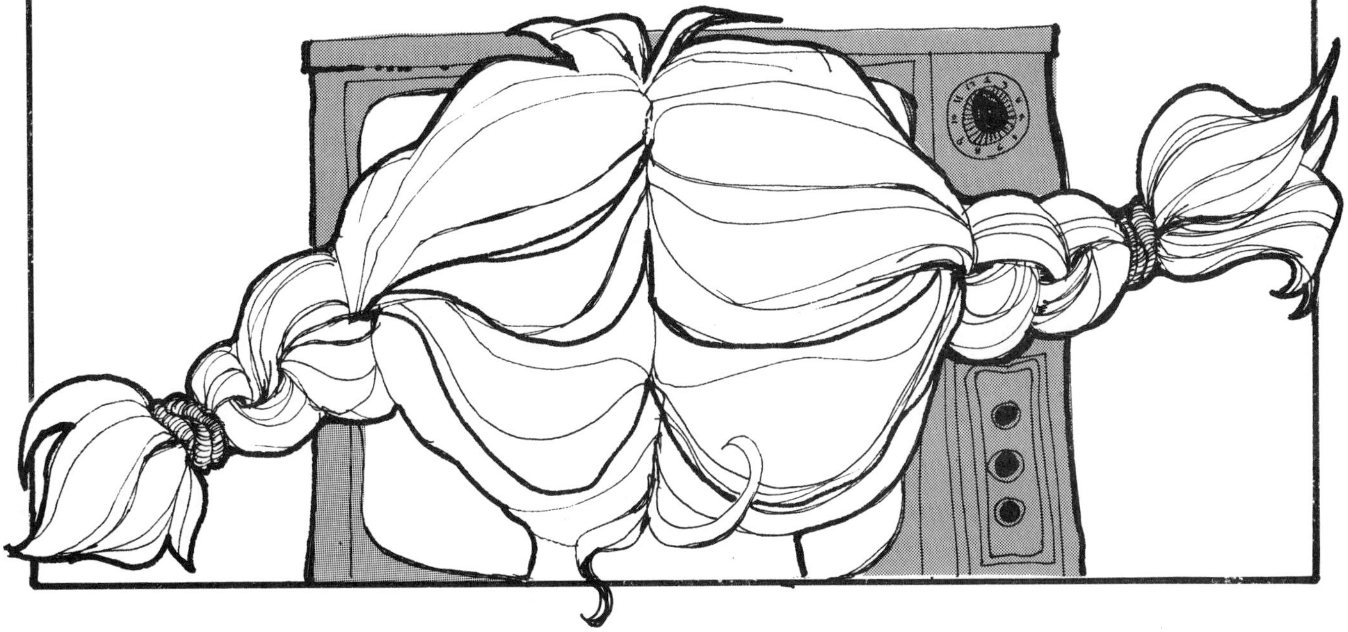

LIBRARY RESOURCE CENTER INVENTORY

Name _____ Date_____

1. Do you like to read? _____

_____

2. What is your favorite book? _____

3. Did you ever read a book more than one time? _____ What was it? _____

_____

4. Do you go to the library with your parents? _____

How often? _____

_____

5. Did you ever ask a librarian for help when you wanted to find something

special? _____What was it? _____

_____

6. Did you ever see a movie of a book that you read? _____ What was it? _____

_____

7. What book did you read that you didn't like? _____

_____

8. I like to read books about

_____ sports	_____ children
_____ animals	_____ adventure
_____ mystery	_____ scary things
_____ fantasy	_____ folk tales
_____ fairy tales	_____ real people
_____ poetry	_____ other people
_____ other places	_____ science fiction
_____ art	_____ science
_____ funny things	_____ friendship
_____ characters from TV	_____ families

Scary Things

TEXTBOOK REVIEW

Name _____

Name of Textbook _____

List four favorite parts or chapters.

1. _____
2. _____
3. _____
4. _____

List one part that looks interesting but that you presently know very little about.

_____

_____

What things are covered in this book that you have studied about before?

1. _____
2. _____
3. _____
4. _____

Find a picture in this book that is very interesting to you. Draw a picture like it on a piece of paper. At the bottom of the paper, give a hint to others that would help them know something about the picture.

Write a brief note that will be sent home to your parents telling about this subject, this book, and the things you will be studying this year. You might include a complete table of contents.

WHO IS IN MY CLASS?

When you get a new group of children you always wonder what they will be like. The children are wondering the same thing about you and about each other. This section is one designed to help you get to know the children, to help the children get to know you and to help them get to know each other.

Things for you to do before the children arrive:
1. Read the list of children's names over and over to yourself so that you are familiar with the first names and the last names. This will help you when you do meet the children.

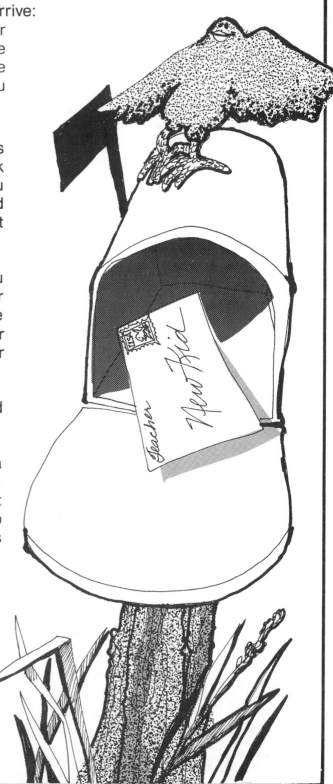

2. Make a name card for each child's desk. You shouldn't put it on the desk before the child arrives unless you have adjustable desks. Luck would have the tallest child in the shortest desk.

   Print or write the name the way you would like to have the child print or write it. Use sentence strips for the younger children and lined paper for the olders ones. Laminate them or cover them with Con-Tact paper.

3. Phone each child before school and chat with him.

4. Mail a letter to each child and include a list of his classmates, a little about you, some of what he will be learning about and a list of things that you want him to bring that first day or week besides traditional supplies (magazines, photos).

WHO AM I?

Building a positive self-concept in children is one step toward self-discipline and good classroom management. Children who feel good about themselves are ready to make friends and are ready to work. This doesn't just happen. It takes time and planning on your part. Try to have one self-concept activity weekly throughout the year and at least one self-concept activity daily the first week. Here are some for starters.

Head of the Class

Each child takes his turn coming in front of the class and starting the timer for two or three minutes. The directions to the child are:

1. You may answer only yes or no to the questions asked.
2. When the time is up, the class must write the information they have gathered in paragraph form. (For younger children you should use chart paper and record the information for them.)
3. All the paragraphs then are given to the child who was at the front of the class, and the decision is made by that child as to which paragraph contains the most accurate information.
4. A reward may be given once to each child contributing the most accurate paragraph.

Each child should have the opportunity to be at the head of the class for examination. And be sure to save all the wonderful paragraphs that are written.

1. Make a copy of the best paragraph. Save these paragraphs from each of the children and make them into a book to have in the reading corner. Each child can draw a self-portrait to be placed opposite the paragraph.

2. Staple all the paragraphs written about the child and have the child make a cover for that book. Illustrations can be supplied during free time by the child or can be done before the paragraphs are handed in each day.

John is cool. He likes to fish, paint, and he loves to roller skate. He is good friend.

Detective on the Scent
The teacher places scratch and sniff stickers on the backs of the hands of students as they arrive, making sure that there are only two of each "scent." After all the students are settled, each student must find another student who has the same "scent." The two students must go to a place in the room and learn everything they can about each other so that they can introduce each other to the group. This activity may be timed as necessary for each grade level.

As I Think—I Am!
This activity is more in-depth and probably should not be done at the beginning of Who Am I activities.

Print several words on the chalkboard, words that evoke emotion: *war, marriage, crime, divorce, separation, homecoming, vacation,* etc. You may choose to put emotion words up for the little children: *love, hate, fear, loneliness, sadness, anger, happiness, concern, worry, anxiety.*

Give each child an 11'' x 14'' piece of poster board, one magic marker or black crayon, and various magazines and newspapers. Have the children cut out pictures, words, phrases, etc., that best describe the emotions that they have chosen. Put them together into a collage to share with the class. Use the magic marker to label, underline, enclose, etc.

Extension Activity
Have the children write paragraphs about experiences when they felt these emotions. Post the paragraphs and the posters together and use them throughout the room.

Have each child select a book that he likes to read that expresses one emotion. Have him paraphrase the story, illustrate the story, make a mock cover for the book and post with the collage.

Try:
Horrible Hepsibah
Alexander and the Terrible, Horrible, Awful Day
Will I Have a Friend?
Hi, Cat   *The Fat Cat*
The Secret Hiding Place   *Cinderella*
Marshmallow   *Play with Me*
Sylvester and the Magic Pebble   *Freckle Juice*
Peter's Chair   *Millions of Cats*
Whistle for Willie   *Crictor*
Whose Mouse Are You?   *Amigo*
Frederick   *Just Awful*
Madeline
Ferdinand

SNIFF
SNIFF

Patches at Work

Collect an assortment of 5'' x 5'' pastel cotton patches. On the first day of school, give students an opportunity to select squares and with felt-tip markers make drawings of themselves on the cotton patches. Place a piece of fabric over each square and iron the colored cotton patches. Remember to make a square with the teacher's name, the school, the grade, and the year. The patches can be used in a variety of ways:

1. Squares can be backed with fiberfill and sewn onto a quilted background.
2. Squares can be sewn together in various shapes and then backed with a sheet of fiberfill and a piece of plain fabric to make a quilt hanging or a blanket for a housekeeping area.
3. After the squares are sewn together, the teacher can make them into a skirt or an apron to be worn on special occasions. (The patches might have to be 12'' x 12''.)
4. Ask the other children in the building to do the same thing and combine all the patches for a hanging for the hallway.

Give the Class Their Roots

Enlarge a world map to create the background for this bulletin board.

Students are to design family coats of arms and determine the countries of origin of their ancestors. They are then to write two unusual facts about ancestors on paper ribbons attached to buttons and place the buttons on the world map.

Each coat of arms is placed around the world map, and a ribbon connects the coat of arms to the place of origin. A school picture can be put near the coat of arms and connected to the second country of origin.

Extension

During the second week have the children bring in treats from family recipes that are suggestive of the countries of origin.

The next week children can play music and display art from their countries.

At another time have them bring in crafts and dress of their countries.

Older students can read about the countries and give reports about weather, climates, traditions, occupations, etc.

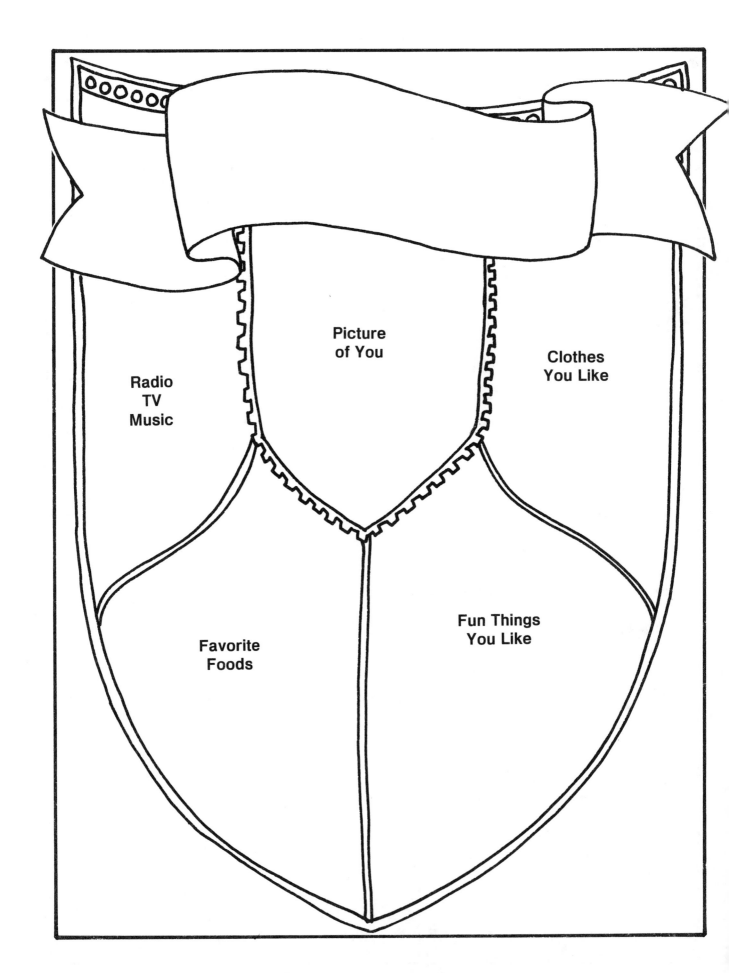

Radio
TV
Music

Picture
of You

Clothes
You Like

Favorite
Foods

Fun Things
You Like

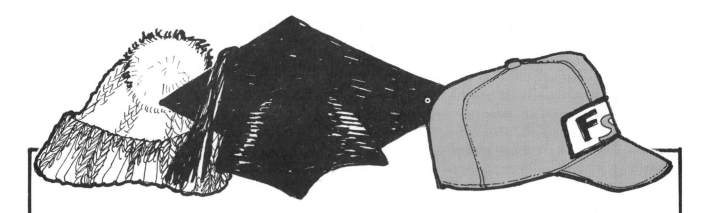

Hi Hats

Have children bring in an old hat from home to introduce themselves to the class. The hat can show a special interest (baseball) or occupation (conductor). As a child goes to the front of the room, the children in their seats can ask questions or listen attentively as the person tells about his hat.

For the children who have no hats, miniatures can be created with items from a hobby, achievement badges, etc. Anything goes, so be creative.

Unlicensed Drivers

Bring in several license plates from different states. Photograph them on your vacation this summer, or ask relatives in various states to send their old ones to you.

After the children have seen what the license plates contain (name of the state, a county indicator, a picture, numbers, etc.), have them design life-sized license plates that represent themselves.

1. Use the model provided on the next page.
2. Measure the plates in your city. Have the children trace around or measure pieces of cardboard the right size. Spray paint them with chrome paint. Put colored library tape around the plates as a border for the license-tag holders. Let the children cut out descriptions of themselves to place on the license tags. They can be two-dimensional for the younger children and three-dimensional for the older children.
3. Place the tags on a bulletin board or on the front of the children's desks with two-way carpet tape.

LICENSE PLATE—DECORATE ONE FOR YOURSELF.

Pairs That Measure Up

Have students get in pairs and trace the outlines of their bodies on large white paper. Then have them paint facial features and clothing on the body outlines. Each child measures his shoe, waist, neck, arms, legs, height, etc., with a tape measure and records the information on the self-portrait.

The portraits are cut out and saved by using clothespins to attach them to a coat hanger. They can be hung in the room along the windows and then stored in a dry cleaning bag until spring.

In the spring, measures are taken again and compared in order to see how each child measures up.

It's Your Day—Hooray!

This activity helps introduce each child to the class. One child is selected to be the student of the day or week. (This selection can be done in a variety of ways: alphabetically, names in a hat, numbers drawn, the one chosen choosing the next, blindfolded child choosing the next from a circle formed around the room.) As a model, you can begin with the Teacher of the Year and bring things about you from home and place them at the front of the room.

The student is encouraged to bring things from home that tell about his life—baby pictures, favorite toys, a pet, food or snack that is his favorite. The class as a whole interviews the child to gain information, and the teacher helps the class develop an experience story based on the information gathered.

Extension

1. Have the children write individual stories, illustrate them and give to the child of the day (week) in book form.
2. Have an assortment of materials from which the children can make portraits of the special child—buttons, rickrack, yarn, thread, pieces of material, etc.
3. Encourage mirror-like images in the portraits by asking the children to draw the child as the child poses for the portrait.

Guess Who

Have the children fill out questionnaires about themselves. Each day pull one questionnaire from the pile and read one statement at a time until the children can guess who the child is.

Cando Strips

Crepe paper streamers are strung from a high wire to the floor to serve as an interim report to the first and second grade parents. Each time parents bring their children into the room, they can check the Cando Strips.

The teacher backs a picture of the child with construction paper and laminates it. The picture is stapled to the top of a streamer and becomes that child's Cando Strip. As the children master emergency information (phone, address, workplace of parents, baby-sitter, etc.), they cut out a symbol, place the information on the symbol and staple it to the strip. Additional curricular information may be added, such as colors, addition facts to ten, etc. When the strip is filled top to bottom, it is sent home with the proud parents.

Getting acquainted with others is not always easy. Some people attend small schools in small towns where everyone knows one another, and you always know the children you are getting. Others live in large cities where teachers never know the children they will have from one year to the next. And then there are those highly mobile areas where, at the end of the year, a teacher might have only ten of the twenty-five she started the year with.

Name games can be played at any time of the year but are especially important at the first. They are also useful when new children arrive.

Pick a Name
Put a name tag on each child. Have each write his name on a card and put it into a container. Choose one child to pick a card from the container and deliver it to the person whose name appears on the card. Each introduces himself, and the one whose name appears on the card picks the next name.

How Do You Do?
Play this game outside. It resembles Drop the Handkerchief. Have the children make a large circle and remain standing. Choose one child to start. (It could be the game starter from the helper chart.) Have the game starter walk around the outside of the circle and stop behind one person and say, ''Hi, I'm Seth.'' The other child turns around and says, ''Hi, I'm Darcy.'' They then shake hands saying, ''How do you do, how do you do, how do you do?'' Each then runs opposite ways around the circle repeating the ''How do you do's'' when they meet halfway. First one back to the origin is the walker. The game goes on.

My Name Is
Have the children sit in a circle in their chairs in the classroom or on the floor in the gym. Have the game starter begin with ''My Name is Paul and I like _____ (any *thing* liked). The child to the left says, ''His name is Paul and he likes _____. My name is Jean and I like _____.'' And so on around the circle.

Variations
Say the name only for the little ones.
Say your name and an adjective that describes you.
Say your name and an adjective that describes you that begins with the same letter as your name.

Name Names
Set the timer to go off at various times during the day and challenge a student to name all the children in the room (or try it yourself).

At each transition time, ask a different child to call the names of the children to get in line.

Scavenger Hunt

Provide each child with the following list of questions and set aside ten minutes for them to find and record the answers. As you make the list of questions, you might want to make several lists that are not all in the same order, or provide only three questions for each child and different questions for everyone or every three people.

Whose name begins with *C?*
Who is the tallest person in the class?
List the names of five girls in the class.
List the names of five boys in the class.
Who wears braces on their teeth?
Who lives nearest the school?
Who visited their grandparents this past summer?
Whose parents have a red car?
What are the names of the children you don't know?
Who has on a dress?
Who has on a green shirt?
Who has a ribbon in her hair?
Whose mother is a teacher?
Who lives with their grandparents?
Who has a sister?
Who has five sisters?
Who has a big dog?
Who is wearing Nikes?
Who played baseball this past summer?
Who played softball this past summer?
Who went to the lake?
Who went to the ocean?

After the children have gathered their information, let them choose one person from their list to give the information to the class.

If you have room in the classroom, put up a 12'' x 18'' piece of construction paper for each child and glue her photo in the corner (see Camera Capers, page 38.) Have each child who has interviewed another child and gathered information about her record that information on the piece of construction paper.

Who's Missing?

Blindfold one child and ask one child to leave the room. Have the blindfolded child guess who is missing. As the children get good at the game, also have them change seats as the child leaves.

Hangman

Play Hangman with the children's names. Start out with first names and go to whole names.

BACK TO THE BASICS

MOTIVATING ACTIVITIES

Effective teachers know that learning must have meaning to children. Although specific skills must at times be taught in isolation, they will best be learned in context. In other words children learn best to read by reading, to write by writing, to create by creating, to understand money by counting and using money, to understand nature by growing plants, raising pets, and interacting in other ways with their environment, to appreciate the social studies by living with the people and issues in their own communities.

The following are ideas that may be part of the first week in order to motivate the children, but should also be a part of a classroom environment that encourages meaningful interactions for all children throughout the school year.

Getting Back to Reading
Sell a book a day to your kids. Read at least 180 children's books that are for children the age you teach. For each book, give a good commercial to sell the kids on that book. (Read Jim Trelease's *Read Aloud Handbook.)*

Read good books to the children. Choose your favorite to start with.

Keep class records of books read by forming bookworms, each segment containing a child's name and the book that he read.

Get a large empty branch to have in the room. Staple leaves on the tree for each book report given to the group.

Present books in drama. Invite parents, other classes, grandparents, school staff, or local preschool classes in to see a presentation.

Create a Book Talk Club. Let the children have time to discuss books in depth, either ones that are preselected and already read or in preparation for the reading of a new book.

Getting Back to Writing
Make spaces and opportunities for sharing writing that the children have done. Let children read their stories to each other.

Keep booklets of class writings on various topics available in the reading corner or center.

Develop a class or school literary magazine to be sent home to parents periodically throughout the year.

Release helium balloons with messages attached.

Write to grandparents or relatives thanking them for visits.

Plan a motivating activity prior to beginning a writing assignment:
  Go on a quiet walk around the school—inside or out.
  See a film.
  Listen to a symphony.

Have children draw pictures of some exciting things and exchange pictures for creative writing experiences.

Cut out paper of different shapes and have them write their stories on elephants, houses, eggs, balloons, dolls, etc.

Getting Back to Spelling
Label yourself. Name your clothing (shirt, socks, shoes), your visible body parts, (palm, sole, fingernail, etc.). Have the children copy and use the words and assign them as spelling words for the first week.

Develop a list of words for the children to know for the first month that includes the names of the other children, the teachers they will have, the school, staff, and parts of the school.

Have spelling team games rather than spelling bees where only one person wins (see Games for Reviewing Skills, page 63).

Getting Back to Math
Do estimating activities. Estimate how many marbles in a jar, chocolate chips per cookie, raisins in a bowl of cereal, raisins per flakes, and then count—and then eat (not the marbles, of course).

Guess how many containers one cup of unpopped corn will take up when popped. Record guesses and actual results.

Graph the number of birthdays per month or the teeth lost (see Tooth Fairy charts, page 24).

Measure each child's height and weight and record that with other vital statistics (see Pairs That Measure Up, page 57).

Do timed tests of very easy skills. Let children succeed.

Place calculators and calculator activities out for the children to do.

Getting Back to Science
Place a set of scales in the room and a large bowl of objects to be estimated, weighed, matched in weight to other objects, etc.

Get a large farm tub and fill it with water and set a large box of objects next to it to test for ability to sink or ability to float.

Set up one aquarium with water and one with soil for use soon.

Approach a local pet shop about having a Pet a Month or ask the children to bring theirs to share with the group.

Show the children how to fill a glass half full of water, place a piece of paper over it, turn it upside down and let go of the paper. Place these materials and other liquids and papers at a center for experimentation.

Getting Back to Social Studies
Remember that all the activities in Who Is in My Class fit here.

The community is a great resource. Write thank-you's for summer programs.

Place a map in the classroom of the area, state, or United States and have the children locate where they spent part of their summer.

Play Community Trivia.

Bring in mystery photos of various places in the community. Have children guess or look for the places throughout the year.

GAMES FOR REVIEWING SKILLS

Games are great for reviewing skills while motivating children. Many can be played with little advance planning and become great "fillers."

Stump the Stars
Hang a cutout television frame for the "star" to stand behind. Classmates try to stump the "star" by asking math facts, spelling words, content questions, etc., that they know the answers to. When the "star" misses, the child who asked the question becomes the new "star," provided he knows the correct answer.

Around the World (Math)
One child stands by a seated child. The teacher gives a math fact. Both children attempt to answer. The child who answers correctly first moves on to the next child, and the child who missed remains at the desk. The winner is the first child to go "around the world" and back to his own seat.

Trivia
Make two lists of review questions. Divide the class into teams. Draw two pictures or shapes on the board divided into an equal number of numbered spaces. Number each set of questions. Teams take turns choosing a number and trying to answer the corresponding question. If correct, the child colors in the numbered space. If not, a child on the other team gets the question. The first team to fill all spaces is the winner.

Checking Checkers
Put math facts or other review questions on the playing spaces of a checkerboard. The child must answer correctly before landing on a square. This can be played by pairs of children, or an overhead transparency can be used for team play.

Quiz Bowl

During the school year fill a plastic fishbowl with cards that have questions (and answers on back) for all curriculum areas. As a filler, quiz the children by drawing questions from the fishbowl. Let the children use the bowl during center and free times. At the end of the year, challenge the parents to the Quiz Bowl challenge. Their children may know more than they do.

And Then the Boiler Burst

All children except one are seated. There is no chair for the child standing. That child tells things that he knows about a given curriculum area and unexpectedly will say the words "and then the boiler burst." That is the signal for each child to change seats while the information giver sits in a vacated seat. The child without a seat becomes the new information giver.

Content Sports

Draw a baseball diamond, basketball court, or football field on the board—if you cannot do this, a child probably can. Divide the class into teams. Prepare questions for content areas to be reinforced. Use Ticky Tack attached to cutout baseball, basketball, or football to move according to game rules. Start in midcourt and toss a coin to see who gets to move first toward which end. The ball then moves only in response to correctly answered questions. If a missed question is answered correctly by the other team, the ball becomes theirs and heads in the other direction. They continue until they either get a field goal (two points) or a touchdown (six points), etc. The ball is then placed in the middle again and goes to the other team.

What Do You Know That I Don't

Pick a subject area for review. Prepare a list of topic words. Divide the class into teams of three to four students. Each team needs paper, pencil, and a person to record.

Write a topic word on the board. Each team in a stated time period lists as many facts about the topic as they can remember. When the time is up (keep very brief), each team in turn lists its recorded facts. Duplicates among teams must be crossed off each team's list. Teams receive one point for each correct fact and two points for each fact that no other team listed.

We're a Pair

Pair children up to practice math facts, spelling words, or what have you. Quiz the children. Reward the partner for a child's correct answers. Children will work harder to help each other learn.

Ticket Out the Door

Before leaving the classroom for lunch, bathroom, home, specials, etc., ask the children questions prompted by tickets clipped to the door. Each child must answer correctly before leaving the room. Questions may be directed to individuals or to the class. For example: How many days in October? How many months in a year?

The Scientist Says

This game is played with the same rules as the game Simon Says. In this game, however, the leader substitutes "Scientist Says" for "Simon Says." This is an excellent technique for studying the 206 bones of the human body, the body parts, and the muscles.

Write On

Word webbing can do wonders for timed, creative writing. The class chooses a familiar topic (swimming, baseball, fairs) to write about for a three to four-minute time period. When the timer goes off, pencils are put down, and a line is drawn under the paragraph to indicate the end of the thought.

Next, the teacher writes the chosen topic on the chart or chalkboard.

The children are asked to think of everything they can associate with the chosen topic before another two or three minutes elapse on the timer. As the timer is set, the students are encouraged to be fluent and verbalize the first thought that comes to their minds. Their ideas are recorded by the teacher as quickly as possible on the board or the chart. When the timer rings signifying an end to the generation of ideas, the students are asked to look at the word web and write a second paragraph about the same topic in an additional three minutes.

At the end of this timed paragraph, children read their first and second paragraphs aloud—one at a time, of course. After listening to all of the paragraphs, the class votes for the most interesting one.

Jeopardy

Make up a list of questions on a topic from last year's curriculum on 6'' x 6'' pieces of oaktag or construction paper. Give them different point values, 5, 10, 20, 30, 50, and 100. Put them up on the chalkboard or bulletin board in five rows forming six columns. The columns are labeled for the number of points given for correct answers.

Form two teams in the classroom, making sure that you balance the two with high and low learners. Continue to play, following the rules of Jeopardy.

YEARLONG ACTIVITIES

These activities are ones that you can start, and the children can work on throughout the year. They can go on and on and on and on . . . .

Journals

Give each child a personal journal on the first day of school. Wallpaper makes a great cover for folded blank sheets, or many stores offer spiral notebooks for as little as $.17 before school starts.

Include a first message to each student.

Dear _____,

This is your journal. You may write anything you wish in it. I am the only person who will read it. I will also write back to you.
You can write about school, home, friends. You can share fun or funny things. You can share sad things and what might be bothering you. I will "listen." You may even ask me questions.

Have fun writing!

Ms. Beveridge

Date each entry. Respond within a day. A child is motivated to write by knowing that you will read and respond. Filled journals will be saved by many children for years to come. The investment in your time pays off in the communication between you and your students.

This Is Our Community

Make a bulletin board of your community using photos that you took during the summer and a city map as the background. Attach to each picture a piece of yarn and thumbtack the end to the correct location on the community map. Include a basket of mystery photos—close-ups of familiar objects or places in the community. Have the children try to identify them.

Spelling Dictionaries

Make a twenty-six-page booklet for each student. Either you or the child write a letter of the alphabet in order on each page. This becomes each child's own personal dictionary. A child must see if the word is in the dictionary before asking for help with it. You could have words missed on spelling tests put in the dictionary. As the dictionaries fill, they become a more and more valuable asset.

Telling a child to "study" his spelling words is not enough. You have to teach a method for studying them. Teach a method, practice it at school, send copies of it home so that parents will know how their children should study their words, and put a copy of the process in the front of each child's *Spelling Dictionary*.

Homework Charts

Homework charts are a great motivation for children to complete the homework or reading away from the school. Each child takes a homework chart home—a chart in the shape of a house that is marked in bricks, each depicting fifteen minutes. Each time fifteen minutes of work is done the parent allows the child to color in a brick and initial it. When the whole house is colored in, the chart is returned and the child receives a reward—see 50 Rewards, page 93.

SSR or DEAR or DIRT

Introduce a Sustained Silent Reading time for everyone in your class. Set aside a daily time in which everyone reads. No one gets up or talks or does anything else. You might call the time DEAR time (Drop Everything and Read) or DIRT (Daily Individual Reading Time), or have your children make up their own acronyms. Begin with only a few minutes of reading time and work up to as much time as is enjoyed and available. You might even set a timer to go off. Make a sign for your door to avoid interruptions.

Finger Rule

Teach the five-finger rule to help children select books that are not beyond their reading levels. Have each child choose a book that looks interesting, open it to any page, and read. Every time he comes to an unknown word, he puts up one finger. If he finds five unknown words on a page, it is probably too difficult. Put it away until later in the year.

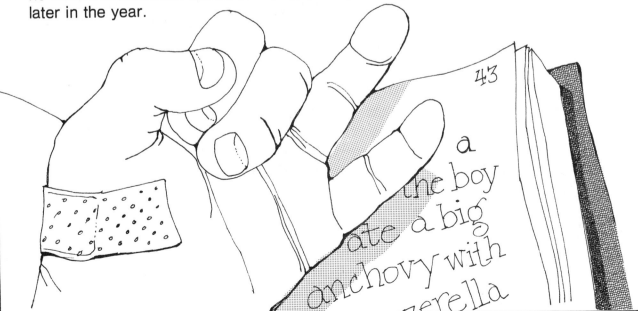

See and Say Books of the Week

On about the third or fourth day of the first week, have the children working in groups of four write a book about their experiences during the first week. Each child can write a different statement and illustrate it. Depending on the level of the child, the statement can be one sentence handwritten or dictated to the teacher. Older children may write paragraphs about one of the experiences that they have had.

Example: First Grade
Page 1: Beth says, "I loved the Autumn Olympiad."
Page 2: Mark says, "My self-portrait is crazy looking."
Page 3: Katy says, "I wonder what will be done with our license plates."
Page 4: Harry says, "I think school is for the birds."

Extensions

Each week have the children do a different book. The books can be done in 4's, 6's, 8's, or the total class.

Topics to consider: Scary Things, Halloween, Our School, The Trip to the Fire Department, The Children's Museum, Caring About Others, We Miss You, etc.

Each different word found in the story can be printed on a page at the back of the book to serve as a glossary.

Books can be written on ditto masters for duplication on various colors of paper.

The books can be used for birthday presents, get-well cards, supplementary reading material for the class or a younger group, invitations, greetings to new children, etc.

Books can follow the topics of the week: About Teeth, What's New in Wichita, All About Alaska, States and Capitals, Families, Friends Are People Who . . ., Magnets, Sinking and Floating, Holidays, Celebrating Christmas Around the World.

UNITS FOR FALL

SUMMER FUN

Let the children share what they did this summer. It will help you get to know them and let them have something to talk about those first few days.

Draw a picture of something you did this summer.

Write a story about something you did this summer.

Write a story about what you did this summer and illustrate it.

Fold three sheets of paper in half. Staple together at folded edge to make a book. Draw one picture per page showing what you did this summer. Write a sentence or two about each picture or ask the teacher to do it for you.

Did you visit a vacation spot this summer? Write a news bulletin about it, selling it to your friends as the most enjoyable place in the world.

Choose one person you visited this summer and write a story about this Most Unforgettable Character.

Choose one community spot you visited frequently this summer and write a thank-you note for having the recreation facility open for your enjoyment. Illustrate your note. Check with the teacher for the mailing address.

Make a collage of magazine pictures about a variety of things that you did this summer.

If you stayed with a baby-sitter for the summer, write a thank-you note, telling about the most fun things that you did.

MYSTERIES OF FALL

A walk in autumn can provide students an opportunity to look for unusual items. As seeds, weeds and plants begin to become prevalent, there is no better time to set out with collection bags.

Give each child a bag in which to collect things. Clear plastic bags are the most language-producing (be sure to give the warnings about using plastic bags), but brown paper bags allow for the most secrecy and intrigue.

Send the children out to collect Mysteries of Fall, making sure that they know they are to look for unusual things, things that are indicative that fall is here. Tell them not to collect more than one or two of any one item. Children can work individually or in pairs.

Much can be done with these mysterious treasures.
1. Have children make collages of all the treasures.
2. Glue treasures onto charts and label what they are.
3. Categorize the treasures by putting all things that are similar together. Make charts for things that are in the same groupings. Label the charts with the group names and then label the individual treasures.
4. Read *The Borrowers* to help children see that their everyday items can be put to unusual uses. Have each then choose his most unusual item, develop a thirty-second commercial and present it to the class. The teacher should encourage students to be original, fluent and flexible as they elaborate upon the values and the benefits of the items chosen. Usable items might include milkweed pods, empty nests, dry flowers or leaves, cocoons, etc.

Have the children present their sales pitches to the members of their own class and then to members of other classes.

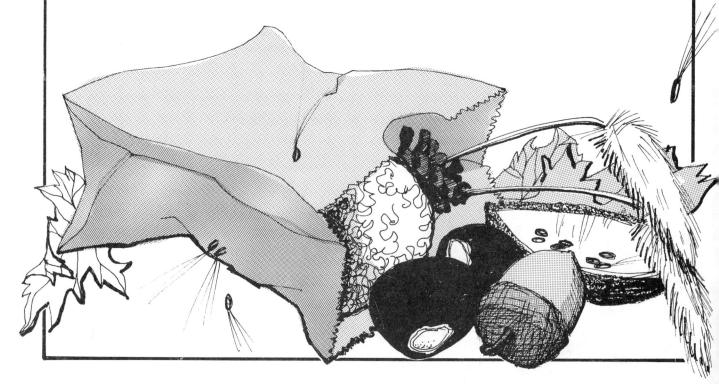

AUTUMN OLYMPIAD

Divide the class into two teams. Adult helpers or aides may assist you in the supervision of each team as they set out to find the following items in one to two hours. (Vary the list as needed for your area of the country and location of your school.)

1. a cocoon/chrysalis
2. a milkweed pod
3. brown fuzzy caterpillar
4. moss
5. five pounds of dry leaves put into a plastic bag
6. three different kinds of seeds from trees
7. an empty home of an animal, bird, or insect
8. an item that begins with each letter in the word *autumn.*

Points may be randomly given for each item and recorded on a large board.

The final event has both teams raking up a very large pile of leaves for the tug of war. A long jump rope is stretched over the leaf pile as students line up behind the team captain. At the sound of the whistle, both teams tug as hard as possible to try to pull the other team through the gigantic leaf pile.

The team with the most points wins and may be rewarded in some manner. All members of both teams then help bag the leaves for use in gardens in the community.

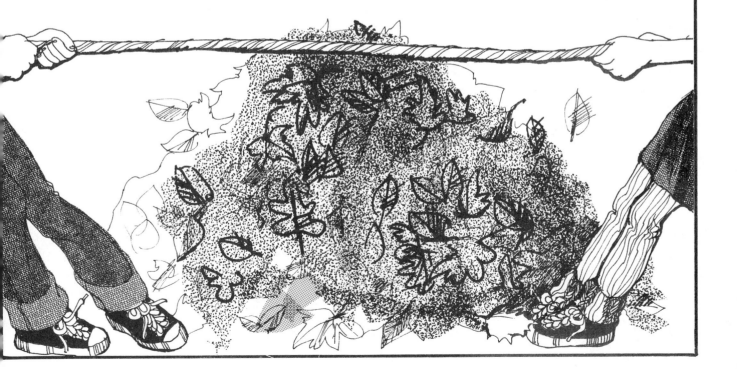

SEEDS, SEEDS, SEEDS

The scattering of seeds is particularly interesting at this time of the year.

Seed Hunt
Send the children out to find various kinds of seeds. Have them go with small bottles of glue, index cards, and pens. When a child finds a seed, he should glue it to a card and record on the back of the card where he found the seed. If he can, have him write what kind of seed it is. If he cannot, have him return to the room and write down the name after investigating to find out what the seed is.

Seed Collage
While children are out on a seed hunt, provide them with small bags in which to put duplicates of seeds that they find. When they return to the room, they can sort the seeds into small muffin tins and use them at an art table to make a collage.

Seed Socks
Ask the children to bring old socks from home—ones that no longer have mates. On a particularly seedy day, let the children put the socks on over one of their shoes. When they return to the classroom, have them plant their socks in gallon milk cartons which have had the tops cut off and have been filled with dirt. Water the socks daily and watch for results.

Seed Sorting
Use the extra seeds that the children collect and provide more seeds for them in a large bowl. Sometimes feed stores or garden stores will let you have a pinch of seed or the seeds left over from spring. Let them sort the seeds onto pieces of paper, into muffin tins, baby food jars, or margarine containers. Learn the names of the seeds and look at the types of plants that they make. The children can sort by colors, shapes, sizes, textures, etc.

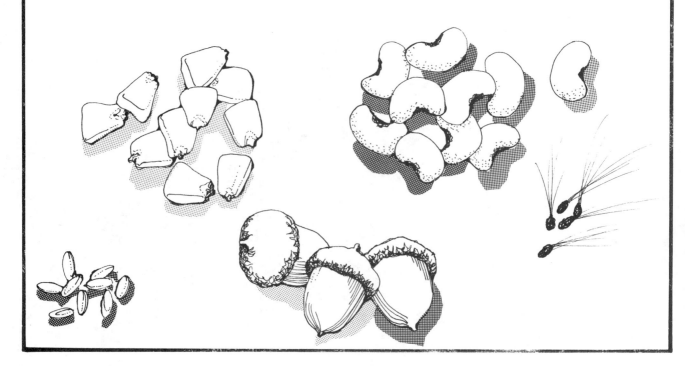

Planting

Plant various types of seeds and take care of them in the room for the winter. Transplant in the spring. Use seeds for experiments.

Place seeds in water and watch.

Place seeds in jars of sand and watch. (Be sure to put the seeds up against the jar.) Water some of the jars and don't water others.

Place seeds in jars of dirt and watch. Follow the directions above.

Split seeds open and see what is inside of them.

Put a cup of seeds into a blender and blend. What happens?

Plant some mystery seeds and see who is the first to guess what common plants the seeds were from.

Seed Scattering

Collect a variety of seeds. Examine them with hand lenses. Try to decide which are scattered by wind, animals, birds, water, other means. Draw a new seed whose design is so good that it is almost guaranteed to be scattered.

Wet a sponge. Sprinkle it with grass seed. Tie a string to the sponge and hang it in a sunny place. Keep it moist and watch the sponge sprout green.

Strong Seeds

Fill a glass jar with lima beans. Fill the jar with water and screw the top on tightly. Set the jar in a covered container and let it stand overnight. Predict what will happen. (The pressure of the beans expanding should break the jar.)

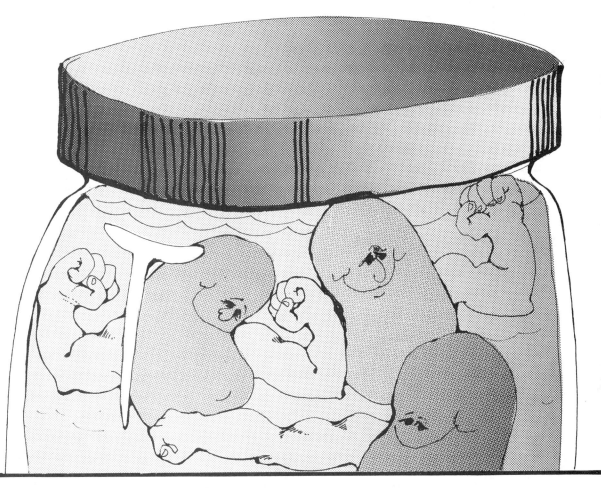

HAPPY BIRTHDAY, JOHNNY APPLESEED

September is the month to celebrate apples, but it is also John Chapman's birthday. He is Johnny Appleseed, you know, and his birthday is celebrated each September 26.

Mark Johnny Appleseed's birthday on the birthday chart.

Have the children write sentences or paragraphs describing an apple and illustrate them.

Check out the stores in your area to see which one carries the widest variety of apples.

Take a trip to the grocery store with the children to see the wide variety of apples that are available.

Purchase one or two of each apple for further use.

When you return to the room and before you bring out the apples that you purchased, have the children once again describe apples. Have them make a comparison of their descriptions before and after.

Display the apples that you purchased. Label each of them. Be sure to get large and small ones; red, green, and yellow ones; different varieties—Winesap, Jonathan, Delicious, etc.

Have the children guess what the apples will look like on the inside.

Cut the apple the traditional way and then cut it around its middle. Have children describe the difference.

Have each child bring a recipe from home—one that his parents use. If they do not use one, have the child name a way that he likes apples and describe how he thinks the apple is processed in order to get that way.

Make apple recipe books that the children can decorate and take home to their parents.

Make some of the recipes that are simple.

Have an apple tasting party—apple butter, dried apples, fresh apples, apple cake, apple pie, applesauce, apple cobbler, fried apples, cinnamon apples, baked apples, apple juice.

Make applesauce.   Make apple juice.   Bake an apple.

Have a Birthday Party
Read the story of Johnny Appleseed. Bring in an old tin pan for a hat and act out the story. There is a film about Johnny Appleseed available in some libraries.

Plant the seeds from the apples that you eat and use for cooking. Seek the help and advice of the local garden store or agriculture department.

BEARS BEFORE HIBERNATION

Children of all ages like teddy bears. Almost all children have them or know someone who does. In fact, most adults have one or want one. They are fun to study about.

Have the librarian hold a library search with a couple of your children to find the books about bears and teddy bears. Make sure that the children learn to keep bears and teddy bears separate in their minds.

Have the children bring their teddy bears to school for the week.

My History of Teddys
Have the librarian find the history of teddy bears for you. Read the history about teddy bears to the children. Have the children write histories of their teddy bears. Then compare what they have written with what you read to them.

Winnie-the-Pooh and Tigger, Too
Read Pooh books and stories with the children. Although there are copies available and illustrated by Shepard and Disney, try reading the books and stories without pictures in order that the children can do their own illustrations. After each story, have the children illustrate their favorite parts. Have them write (or dictate) the narratives that would go along with the pictures. Post them in the hallway in sequential order. People who pass by can read the stories and see the illustrations.

Have the children bring their teddy bears to school for the week.

Teddy the Bear and My Other Friend, Too
Let the children write stories about their teddy bears and one of their other stuffed animals. Put the stories into books, bind them and have the children illustrate them. Photograph the children with their bears for the cover of the book. (Photograph the set of bears and each individual bear for future use.)

The Not-So-Antique Bear Show
Have children bring in their oldest teddy bears and tell about them in a special time, the ''Not-So-Antique Bear Show.'' Bring in one of your old bears.

Teddy Bear's Picnic

Read the *Teddy Bear's Picnic*. If the weather permits, have a picnic for the children and the bears.

"Bery" Own Bear

Have a variety of cloth scraps available. The children can use simple patterns and make clothes for their bears, or they may cut out two pieces of a bear pattern that they designed, stitch around the edges, and stuff it to have their "bery" own bears.

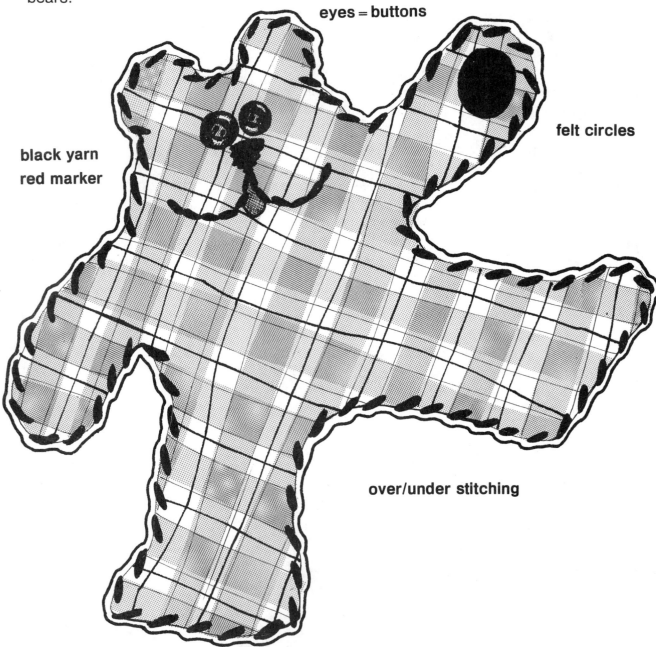

eyes = buttons

felt circles

black yarn
red marker

over/under stitching

Which Bear

Have the children write descriptions of their bears and give them to you. Place all of the bears in their special spots. Mix up the descriptions and have each child come forward to read about one of the bears. Let the children guess which bear it is, making sure that the one whose bear it is is quiet during this time.

SCHOOL SAFETY

Be sure to discuss safety with the children during those first few days and weeks of school. There is so much to discuss; however, don't frighten them.

The Bus

Put up pictures of buses in the room and place children in the windows. Number the buses and put the children's names on the faces in the windows of the buses to show which bus each child is to take.

Be sure that the children feel comfortable finding the bus that they ride.

Have the children write a set of rules for riding the bus.

Have the children write a story about The Crazy Kids on the Crazy Bus. Use this picture as a story starter.

Talk with the children about waiting for the bus in their neighborhoods and near their homes. Make sure they know about waiting calmly and away from the street.

Have the bus drivers come to the room and tell the children about their job and the responsibilities that they have. Let them discuss with the children the rules and the need for them.

Walk the children to the bus daily. Even if this is an extra chore for you, it will keep them calm that far and help the atmosphere on the bus as they enter it.

Safety at School

Visit the rooms in the school that are specifically for safety's sake. Visit the nursing station. Find the first aid kit. Locate the exit signs. Find the fire pulls and the fire extinguishers.

Look for safe things in your school and on the playground.

Look for unsafe things in your school, on your playground, and in the surrounding community. Notify the proper people about the hazards.

Set rules for the children to follow soon. Make sure that you tell them that the rules are for their safety and the safety of others. Remember to have as few rules as possible.

Procedures can sometimes eliminate the need for rules. Perhaps they are rules, but if they are set as procedures, the children don't think they have as many rules to follow.

   Set procedures for hallway walking.
   Establish procedures for bathroom breaks.
   Set procedures for in-house locomotion.
   Set procedures for playground arrival and dismissal.

Stranger Danger

Be sure to talk with the children, stressing that they are not to go home with anyone they don't know or anyone that you don't have permission for them to go home with.

Make sure parents know that you will not allow the child to go with someone you don't know or don't have permission for the child to go with.

Talk about friendly strangers—firemen, policemen, social workers, counselors, etc.

FRIENDSHIP

The beginning of a school year is a perfect time to focus on feelings and friendships. Gather all the books you can find about friends, school, beginnings, feelings. Some tried-and-true books are:

Henry and the Paper Route
Ira Sleeps Over
Will I Have a Friend?
Crow Boy
George and Martha
Frog and Toad Are Friends
Let's Be Enemies
The Velveteen Rabbit

My Friend John
The New Boy on the Sidewalk
Lovable Lyle
Best Friends for Frances
Charlotte's Web
Rosie and Michael
Beverly Cleary Books
Miss Rumphius
Can I Keep Him?

Keep the books close at hand in order to use them at times when needed.

Activities that help children understand friendships and develop friends are many, but a few to try include:

Furry Friends
Write or describe your favorite stuffed animal friend. Bring it to school hidden in a container. Classmates try to guess what your "friend" is from the clues in your description.

Kinderfriends
Kinderfriends are kindergartners and "older" school friends who buddy up for reading stories, working on projects, talking and listening, practicing skills.

Wanted: A Friend
Write a classified ad to find the perfect friend. Include all the qualities and interests you want in a friend. Put the ads in a class mailbox. Draw an ad and answer it, pretending you are the very person the ad writer is looking for.

Friendship Circle
Have the children sit in a circle and choose a special class stuffed animal. Hold the animal yourself and say something nice about one of the people in the class. Pass the animal to that person who says something nice about someone else. Continue until something positive has been said about everyone in the room.

Good Friend Awards

Run off copies of the Good Friend Award and make them available for children to use to show their awareness of friendship. Each time someone befriends them, they can fill out one of the Good Friend Awards. The awards can be posted in the classroom for a certain period of time and then taken home to share with parents. These awards give children the opportunity of putting positive feelings towards others into words even if they are unable to say these things to the person directly.

Catalog Gifts

Give children catalogs. Have them choose the perfect gift for a friend or for a character in a book about friendship.

Bulletin Board

Take photos of each child and his special friend. It could be a classmate, teacher, parent, adult friend, stuffed animal, doll, pet, etc.

Songs

Check the Marlo Thomas album on friendship.
''It's a Small World''
''Make New Friends''
''Reach Out and Touch Somebody's Hand''
''Love Makes the World Go Round''

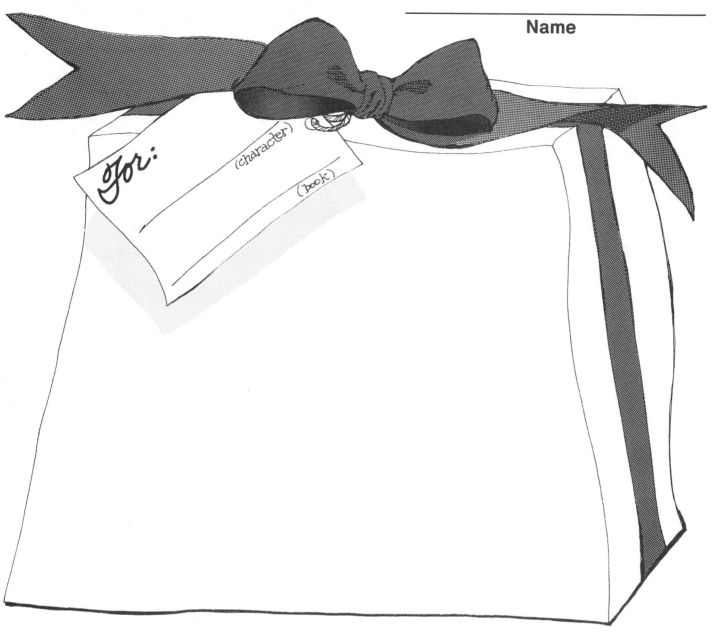

For:

(character)

(book)

Directions: Pretend you are a friend of someone in a book. What would your friend most like to have?
1. **Draw or write it in the gift box.**
2. **Write two or more sentences telling why it is the perfect gift.**

_____

_____

_____

_____

_____

_____

_____

GARBAGE

Garbage/trash/litter is something we all have and all have seen. Children need to become aware of garbage and trash and what to do with it in order not to litter. They need to learn to keep their own areas free of garbage and trash and as they get older to know how to keep their school, home areas, and communities free of litter. This unit will help with those skills.

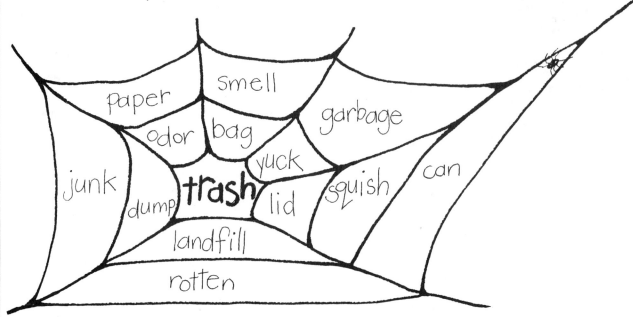

Creative Writing

Introduce the concept of webbing to the children. There are several definitions of webs: 1. A spider spins a web to collect food. 2. Some animals have webs on their feet to help them collect water pressure to swim faster. 3. A web holds things together.

Draw a large web on a piece of poster board. Make it have enough boxes so that the children are challenged to fill it in the four minutes that they will be given.

Today I am going to say one word and write it in the center of the web. When I say the one word, I want you to tell me all of the words that it makes you think of. I will give you only minutes, and we need to fill the whole web. The word is *trash.*

Students call out words and the teacher fills the boxes. An aid can help if necessary.

Examine the words that the children have given. Look for nouns, adjectives, verbs, adverbs and compound words.

Have the children write their own paragraphs about trash using the web of words as their word bank. Encourage the children to elaborate upon an idea to make it more exciting. Discourage them from listing ideas from the web.

If the children are a bit older, once again set the timer for four minutes to encourage more fluency and generate more creative ideas.

Math

Divide outdoor area around the school into one, two, three, or four sections. Students are to take a litter walk. Children take with them a magic marker to date the litter that they find. They then return it to where they found it, disturbing it as little as possible. On a clipboard a litter ditto is clipped, and children record information about the litter for future reference.

Section	Date	Description of Litter

One Week Later—Return to the same area with the students. Have them look for the litter that they had previously recorded on their dittos. If the litter is still visible, record it again on the ditto sheet marked **One Week Later.**

Two Weeks Later—Return to the same area with the students continuing the process.

Upon return to the school have the students:
1. Categorize the litter as metal, biodegradable, paper, plastic, etc.
2. Create a bar graph to disseminate information you have produced as a researcher. Ex: What trash was still on the ground after one week, two weeks, etc.
3. Have the students disseminate this information to other classes, P.T.A., the board of education, staff meetings, a school assembly, etc.

Art—Trash Family

Collect trash for a few weeks.

Empty trash outside in one corner of the school grounds. Have the students sort the trash and categorize it (science).

Have the students choose one family member to construct a life-sized model out of trash. Three or four students may be working together to construct the brother, sister, mother, dad, pet, etc. This family may be displayed in the town library for Litter Prevention Week.

Mini Center

Use two pieces of railboard to make a standing, folding, portable center. Tape them together with duct tape and cover them with Con-Tact paper. Put duct tape around the edges.

Place a large beautiful picture of garbage in the corner and title your center "Garbage: What Is It? What Should I Do?"

Put up six hooks, velcro circles, or pockets on the center. For each of the hooks, make a card that has on it one of the following activities:

1. List recycled trash items. Create a picture cube from your list.
2. Explain the step-by-step process of recycling aluminum cans.
3. Collect pictures or take photographs of a landfill. Make a collage or display.
4. Analyze a bag of trash from your neighborhood. What can you learn about that family that is different from yours?
5. Create a monster out of the trash you have collected. Write about its unique attributes.
6. Judge the safety of burning trash at home. Support your answer with at least two reasons why you feel the way that you do.

Science

Question: How does mold dispose of waste in nature?

Observation: Bread of all kinds kept in various places.

Research: List things you know and those things you want to find out. Research and read about mold. Define new terms you come across.

Hypothesis: Make a guess toward your answer based on what you have observed.

Experiment: Design an experiment or replicate an experiment to prove or disprove your hypothesis.

Data Collection: Make several observations about your experiment. Record the observations in writing or through illustrations or photographs.

Conclusions: Analyze findings. Was your hypothesis proven? Disproved? Null?

Application: So what? Why is it necessary for anyone to learn about the information you have produced?

SOLVE A MYSTERY

Background—black
Private eye—white with black, red, and yellow
Magnifying glasses—red with clue to Book Talk Book, a portion of the cover of the book is behind each book jacket.
Book jacket for each of the books read during the week.

Build a Body—a takeoff on the game of Cooties

Materials:
a spinner with body parts listed on it
enough of each body part listed so that each student has enough to complete one body
model body for the children to follow
brads
paper punch

Directions:
Object: Be the first to complete a skeleton body following these rules:
1. A specific sequence is required. A player cannot start drawing until he or she gets a "head." The other parts must be attached to a part already received—no hand without getting an arm first.
2. Take turns spinning. A player cannot take a part unless it can be attached.
3. At the end of playing time, any player without skeleton parts may take the needed pieces and complete the skeleton in free time.
4. Only one skeleton to a player. For future playing times, use paper and crayon to draw the body parts.

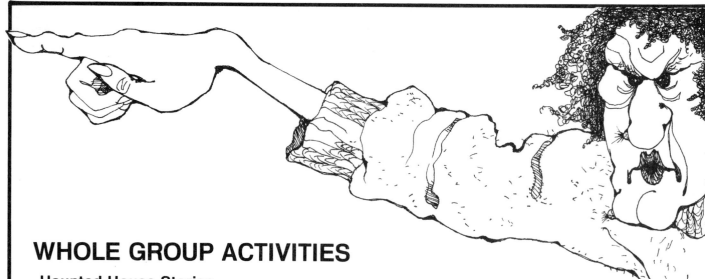

WHOLE GROUP ACTIVITIES

Haunted House Stories
Write haunted house stories. Have the children design haunted houses out of paper and crayons, sticks and stones, wood and glue, etc. Light the houses from within or from behind.

Pull the shades in a dark room. Light the houses and read haunted house stories with a flashlight.

Miss Nelson Is Missing
Read *Miss Nelson Is Missing* to the children early one morning. Get sick yourself about eleven and return to the class dressed as Miss Viola Swamp. Treat the children as Viola does in the story. Have an afternoon of drill, ditto sheets, no fun, formality, homework, etc.

Review *The Day with Miss Viola Swamp* during opening exercises the next morning, and have the children write stories about their experiences with Miss Viola.

Mixed Up Mystery Smell
Use this book to read to the children as you help them learn about how to read, think, predict. Read part of the story, help the children learn to predict using clues from the story, have them reach a conclusion of their own, and then read the conclusion to the story. If you want, you can read only part of the story to the children and use their predictions as the conclusion without reading the actual ending yourself. It will be fun to see how many of them are interested in the "real" outcome of the story.

Peddler's Packs
Decorate lunch sacks for each mystery that you read to the children. Put objects, pictures, and other clues in the sack as you read the story to the children. They can use the sacks and clues to sequence and retell the story to each other or to draw a picture story to go along with the real story that you have read.

SOME CENTER ACTIVITIES

Suspect Alley
Materials: hat, slips of paper with children's names, one paper doll-shaped body
for each child, pencils

Put all of the children's names on slips of paper and put them in a hat on the table. Have each child select the name of a classmate and make secret observations about that person. Each child then records his observations on the body-shaped piece of paper. Have the children post their bodies on a bulletin board entitled Clues to Classmates.

As a whole group activity, one person can read the observation clues and the children can guess who the suspect is.

Fingerprinting
Materials: ink pads of different colors, blotting paper 6'' x 6'' for the whole hand of each child, blotting paper 2'' x 2'' for each finger of the child done already on the 6'' x 6'' paper, ink pens, magnifying glasses

Have each child make a set of fingerprints on a 6'' x 6'' piece of blotting paper and put his name at the bottom of the paper.

Have each child use the same hand and different colors of ink for each of the four fingers and thumb and make prints on the 2'' x 2'' squares of blotting paper. Have the children put a code for themselves, not their names or initials, on the small squares. Put the prints in two separate file boxes.

Children can go to the centers and try to match fingerprints. When they think they have them matched, they are to check with the person they have chosen to match.

Clue
Play Clue.

Who Done It?
Have each child write a story to place in the center and sign his name to the story.

Have the other children try to match their handwriting and signatures.

Let the children write stories and not sign them and see if people can find out "who done it" without using names on the stories.

Code Breakers
Use various pre-purchased code sheets during the week to discover things they are not able to discover readily.

MANAGEMENT

RULES AND CONSEQUENCES

One of the most important things to remember at the beginning of school is that we get these children fresh from a summer's rest, and they are excited about returning to school. We don't even have to motivate them. They are already highly motivated. We just need to keep them excited about school and about learning.

Sadly enough one of the first things we are concerned about when we get a new group is that they know right away that we are the boss, that we have rules and that they will have to follow them. The way we approach this at first can set the tone for the rest of the year. And if we seem too mean or at all unfair, we may lose them for a long time.

All too often children go home remembering how stern we were when we delivered our rules lecture and cannot remember another thing that happened that day. It is probably best to begin the day with fun things to do. Say to them that this class does and will have rules to follow just like any other class has in the past, but you know that they know how to behave and you would like to do some fun things the first few days. Then get around to setting the rules with them and deciding on what the consequences are going to be. If you see that this is not going to work, then you probably need to switch into the rule-setting mode. If you see that it will work, watch your students, get to know them, and then decide what rules you want to generate with them.

Setting Rules
Children work best when they have a hand in making the rules. Start the discussion with something like this:

It is pretty obvious that when there are a lot of people we are likely to need rules for safety and to help us remember not to bother others. Can you tell me some of the things that we should remember to do or not to do?

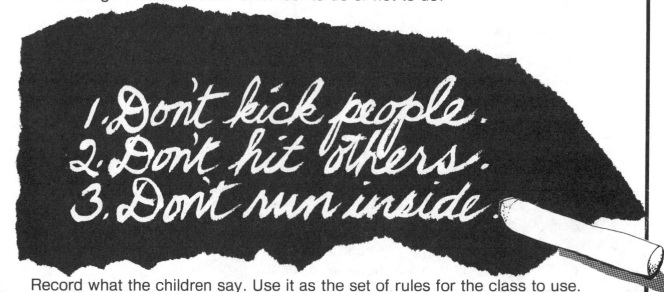

1. Don't kick people.
2. Don't hit others.
3. Don't run inside.

Record what the children say. Use it as the set of rules for the class to use.

Rules

1. Don't kick people.
2. Don't hit people.
3. Don't run inside.

Review the rules daily, and as time goes by, condense them with the help of the class.

Have the children draw pictures to post beside the rules to indicate to you and others that they know what the rules are and to help those who cannot read to "understand" the rules.

Setting Consequences
Let the children decide what might happen to them if they break these rules that they have set. You will be surprised to see that they have some pretty good ideas. Make sure that you can live with the consequences that you and the class decide on. Be sure that you think about each child and what that child's reaction would be if he had to "suffer the consequences."

Once the consequences are set, be consistent and unemotional when telling a child that he has broken the rule. Make sure that he knows exactly what the consequences are and what will happen.

Never Take the Consequences Away
Be caring with the children as you impose the consequences for the infraction. Ask them to do what they are to do and when they have "suffered the consequences," make sure that you help them with a successful reentry into the group's activities.

Suggested Consequences
  a hot seat where they sit for one minute until they can warm up to the group— until they stop giving cold pricklies and begin to give warm fuzzies.

  head down for one minute.

  moving away from the group and turning from them for one minute.

Rules Can Be Posted in Various Ways

Do's and Don't's for Room 7

Be nice.
Be quiet.
Mind your manners.
Follow directions.
Do your own work.
Be kind and helpful.
Pick up messes.
Walk inside.

Don't run.
Don't hit.
Don't bite.
Don't spit.
Don't kick.

REWARDS

Rewards come in all shapes and all sizes. There are ways to reward the group and ways to reward individuals. But one thing you must remember for sure is that you should **never take a reward away from a child who earns it!**

Group Rewards

1. The Marble Jar. This is one that is especially used with assertive discipline. The teacher must look for opportunities to reinforce the group.

   Are they quiet?

   Are they on task?

   Does everyone have his pencil sharp and ready?

   Did they leave the closet neat after recess?

   Every time one of these things occurs, put a handful of marbles in a see-through jar. When the jar is so full that the lid will not fit on, it is time to stop the scheduled day and have a class activity for reinforcement. The reinforcing activity can be a surprise or class-selected.

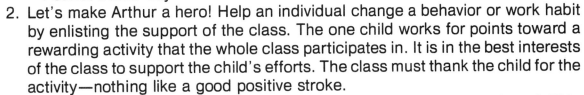

   Try:

   Class game

   Popcorn party

   Free time

   Extra story

   Afternoon recess—all afternoon

   Art

   Music and social time

   Apple day

   Peanut butter day

2. Let's make Arthur a hero! Help an individual change a behavior or work habit by enlisting the support of the class. The one child works for points toward a rewarding activity that the whole class participates in. It is in the best interests of the class to support the child's efforts. The class must thank the child for the activity—nothing like a good positive stroke.

3. Are you listening? Place a scale from one to ten with an ear at each end. Title this chart "Are You Listening?" Each seating group has a cutout symbol that moves along the scale (up and down) in relation to responses to listening and following directions. At the end of the day, the highest group (or all groups that reach a perfect 10) gets a rewarding activity.

Individual Rewards

1. Best Citizens. Any child whose name is not on the board for a week gets a Best Citizen certificate and gets to sign the Best Citizen Book.

2. I'm Special booklets. Give each child a booklet with blank pages and a decorated I'm Special cover. Stamp a page with a special rubber stamp to indicate anything you wish to reinforce. The child can color it, and/or write the reason for the stamp. Ten stamps equal a special reward.

3. Raffle Tickets. Pass out raffle tickets for excellent work, following directions, being helpful or polite, remembering, bringing asked-for items from home, etc. Write the names on the tickets and put in a raffle bucket for the end-of-the-day drawing or have students save a given number of tickets which can be traded for a special privilege—either drawn or chosen (see 50 Rewards on the next page).

4. Give the child a great big bear hug for the things that he does that are satisfying to both him and you.

5. Any time that the child is doing something very special, send home a note to the parents. You can write them or have some cute notes run off on which to write the child's name.

_____

was a rainbow bringer today because _____

_____

50 REWARDS THAT DON'T COST MUCH MONEY OR ROT YOUR TEETH

Sit at the teacher's desk.
Be the zookeeper and take care of the animals.
Have lunch with your favorite person.
Join another class for indoor recess.
Get a free milk.
Have bread and peanut butter at snack time.
Have the teacher phone your parents to tell them what a great kid you are.
Draw on the chalkboard.
Use the clay during free time.

Chew sugar-free gum for the day.
Be the first in line.
Do only half the math assignment.
Choose any class job for the week.
Choose the music for lunch. Bring in a record or tape.
Take a tape recorder home for the night.
Use colored chalk at the board or on a piece of paper.
Do all the class jobs for the day.
Invite a lunch visitor from outside the school.
Work on a mural.

Get a drink whenever you want to.
Use the pencil sharpener any time.
Make a bulletin board.
Put fifteen marbles in the group reward jar.
No early morning work.
Be a helper in another room with younger children.
Help Ms. Parker, the custodian.

Stay in at recess to play a game with a friend.
Use stamps and ink pad.
Write in ink for the day.
Invite a friend from another class into the room for lunch.
Use the teacher's rocker instead of a desk chair.
Work in the lunchroom.
Take home a class game for the night.
Sit by a friend for the day.
Move your desk to the chosen location.
Keep an animal on your desk—stuffed or not stuffed.
No homework pass.
Lunch with Ms. Beveridge.
Operate the filmstrip projector.
Use the couch or beanbag chair for the day
Choose any of the rewards that you want.
Go to another class for lunch.
Use the typewriter.
Be the first to eat.
Use the tape recorder and tape a story.
Have a special sharing time to teach something to the class,
   set up a display, etc.
Be leader of a class game.
Extra center time or extra recess
Read to a younger child.
Read to someone else.

GROUP PROBLEMS

1. Friendship Circle

Sit in a circle. Each child takes a turn telling something specific that someone in the class has done for him that shows friendship. It must be focused on the other person, not the self. The child spoken of gets to hold class friendship mascot—teddy bear or animal not usually played with by children. The friend gets to hold it until another child is called a friend.

2. Settling Problems

Label one chair a listening chair and one chair a talking chair. Take the two children who are fighting or arguing and let them sit across from each other in these two chairs. The children must look at each other. The listener must listen if in the listening chair. The talker talks when in the talking chair. They switch places and roles are switched. The teacher must facilitate the working out of the problem.

3. Come into My ''Private Office''

Upset children like private conversations with a teacher. Privacy is not possible in most classrooms. Invite the child to come with you into your ''private office''—floor space in the hall. The phrase gives recognition to the child of his need to be away from the others. Be a good listener and hear what the child is really saying to you and help solve the problems.

4. Problem Pail

Hypothetical or actual situations which cause children concern or anxiety are written on small pieces of paper and placed into the Problem Pail by the teacher or by students. (It is best if an actual pail can be used.) A designated time is set aside five or ten minutes a couple of times a day or week, whenever convenient or as needed. A student is then chosen to select a problem from the pail, read it and be the discussion leader. (For the younger ones you might have to be the leader a few times first.) It is conducive to good group interaction if the student can assume an informal position on the floor and have the children sit in a circle.

This activity provides an excellent opportunity to deal with current problems which are arising in the classroom or in the school. There must be rules for discussion because arguments might occur.

Listen to the one who is talking. Let him finish before you begin.
Only one person is to speak at a time.
Discuss the problem and why it probably happened.
Try to find several solutions that might be tried.
Select one solution to work on in order to see if it works.
End on a positive note.

TRANSITIONS FOR CREATIVE THINKING

As you get in line to go places, have each child give a different response to these statements:

Name something that is red (or any color).

Name something that is round (or any shape).

Name a number that no one else has named.

Name something that is huge (or any size).

Name something you don't like to eat (or do).

Name something you can do with your feet (or hands).

Name something you like to do after school (or don't like to do).

Name something that flies (or walks or runs).

Name a character in a book (or story, TV show, movie).

Name a math problem that has 8 for an answer (or any other number).

Name a word that begins with *b* (or any letter, blend, digraph).

Name a word that ends with *g* (or any letter, blend, digraph, or ending).

Name a compound word (or contraction, two-syllable, etc.).

Tell your phone number (or address, full name, parents' names, grandparents' names).

Name something living (or nonliving).

Name a bird (or animal, fish, mammal, pet).

Name a piece of clothing (or furniture).

Name a means of land transportation (or air, space, water).

Name a vegetable (or fruit, meat, dairy product).

Name something made of wood (or glass, plastic, material).

Name a game.

Something that flies.

Post this near the door or on your desk.

SUB SURVIVAL KIT

Lettuce look at the rules. See page 1 of this sub sandwich for a list of the rules and their consequences. Go over them with the class.

Meat our room helpers.
The helpers' names for each week are found on page 2 of this sub sandwich.

Mustard up enthusiasm by trying the following brain teasers: Bingo math, spelling bee, creative problem solving. See page 3 of this sandwich.

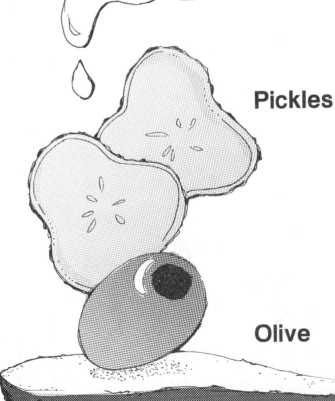

Pickles Keep out of these by:
1. Checking class seating chart
2. Reviewing extra duty roster
3. Observing lunch and recess times
4. Checking bus duty chart. See page 4.

Olive us will have a great day this way.

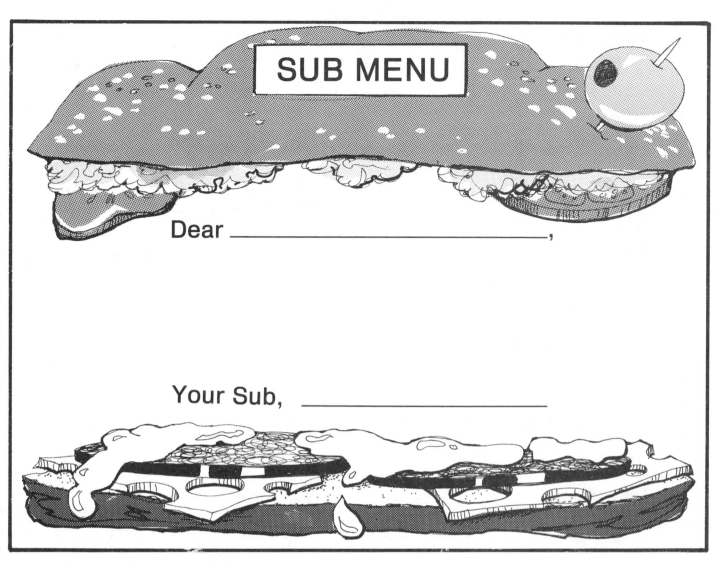

SUB MENU

Dear _____,

Your Sub, _____

Also use Scratch and Sniff stickers in pickle and pepperoni scents. Look for others too!

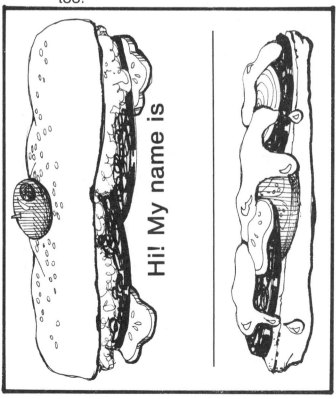

Hi! My name is

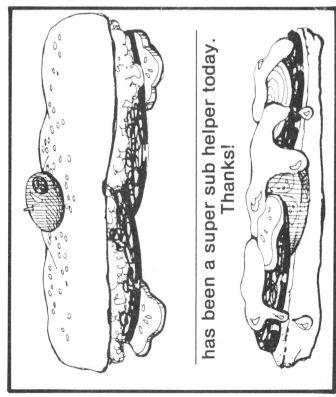

has been a super sub helper today. Thanks!

INFORMING PARENTS

Parents are one of the most valuable resources. You must keep on good terms with them and they with you. The children are in between and they must survive.

WHAT IS HAPPENING IN MY CHILD'S CLASSROOM?

Parents must know what is expected of their children. Most schools do send home their discipline policies and periodic newsletters. However, this does not let parents know what children are learning in school and therefore parents cannot reinforce what is being taught. (Many of you have asked children what happened in school today, only to be told, "Ah, nothing," with a shrug of the shoulders.) Certainly something has to be going on in school. It is your job to keep parents informed about what is going on. Try these this year.

Letters of Welcome
One of the first pages of this book was a letter of welcome to the students. This is a wonderful way to let parents know you really are concerned about their child. Why not try sending a personal note home to the parents, too, that first week.

Come on In
On the first Friday of that first week, plan to have a tea for parents where children can show their parents around and parents can meet you. Open House is a good time for this, but it usually isn't until October. There is a lot of mystery until then.

Subject of the Week
Each week choose one subject that the students have been studying and have them spend five minutes at the end of each day jotting down what they have done in that subject. At the end of the week make a cover for the booklet and send it home for the children to share with their parents.

What I Did This Week
Divide one sheet of white 9" x 12" paper into four parts and give each child four pieces stapled together at one side. This will form a weekly log. Have the child put "What I Did This Week" on the front page (or ditto it on for the little ones at first). On the first page write "Monday," the second "Tuesday," etc. At the end of each day, take five minutes to note what was done for the day. It can be done in pictures for the little ones (use larger paper) and in writing for the older ones. This will also give you some idea of just what the children are remembering.

Parent of the Day
Invite parents to the room for the day. Invite only one parent or set of parents in to visit at a time. Have them stay for thirty minutes, one hour, or a half day. It will depend on your school and parents' schedules. This can be done when their child is Child of the Week, on the child's birthday, or when the parent is used as a resource person. (See invitation, page 23.)

Parent Teas
Have parent teas at various times during the year. It is not necessary to have one each month or even to have more than one or two a year, but do have them. Try the first Friday, Open House, Thanksgiving, Christmas, Valentine's Day, St. Patrick's Day, April Fool's Day, Easter, May Day, or the end of school. Let the children prepare the feast and the table decorations. They may seat their parents, use good manners, serve the tasties, pour the ''tea'' and show their good host/hostess skills.

Quiz Bowls
When the children have finished a unit of study and have answered many questions on a certain subject, invite parents to a quiz bowl and have the children challenge the parents. You might be surprised and so might the parents. Be sure to put in all sorts of trivia that the kids will know and the parents will likely not.

Letters to Parents
After children have written to their parents telling them what is going on in class, have children write letters to their parents and grandparents and ask them to write back to tell what they remember about their kindergarten, first, second, third, or fourth grade experiences. Have the children read their parent letters to others in the class.

Grandparent Day
Have a special day when children can bring their grandparents to school or invite them anytime that they are in town. If children do not have grandparents, an older neighbor would do. It is really good to keep these taxpayers aware of just what good things are going on in the schools.

We Missed You
When children are absent, send notes home with assignments (see next page).

NEWSLETTERS

Pages 101 and 102 have outlines for classroom newsletters. The first one is designed for one room's use, the second for a school's use. Xerox a copy for the children to write on, have them fill in one box, sign it and put little illustrations around the edge. You can have a one-page newsletter weekly, a two-page newsletter biweekly, or more or fewer pages as needed. Make sure that everyone gets a chance.

We missed You!!!

Name_____ Date_____

While you were absent, you missed some work which needs to be made up at school or home and handed in. Please see me if you need help.

Subject	Assignment	✓ when completed

News from Grade

print
grade number
here

Newsline

TIPS FOR TOP CONFERENCES

Parent conferences can be stressful meetings for children and parents. Here are a few tips that might help guide the conferences to being more pleasant and a letter that you might send home to the parents before conferences to help them be prepared for the meeting.

Early Preparation
1. Make a blank file card for each child at the beginning of the year. Keep these handy on your desk and note behaviors, accomplishments, and other notable things on the cards during breaks, lunch, or movies. This serves as valuable documentation about the child and concerns that you might have.
2. Have each child bring an empty notebook at the beginning of the year and keep it in his desk. When you have something you want to say about him, have him bring the notebook to you for a warm fuzzy. (This will help you keep the comments positive. The children will probably toss the negative ones.)
3. Begin file folders at the beginning of the year with children's work to be put in at least weekly. Let the children put in the ones that they want, and you can put in ones that you choose.

Conference Week
1. Send home the note on the next page.
2. Make sure that report cards have gone home and parents have been requested to bring the cards with them to the conference. Be sure that there were no surprises on the grade card. Keep in touch with parents all the time.
3. Put up a table with chairs around it in the hall. On it place the textbooks that you use in your classroom and copies of unused workbooks.
4. Arrange a round table for meeting with the parents. Purchase a nice plant or potted flower to put in the center of the table. Dust your desk and clean the chalkboard trays.
5. Have a timer nearby to warn you that time is almost up.
6. Prepare a list of skills or ideas that each parent might like to work on with his child. Gear them to the child and to the parents.
7. Share something positive with the parents to begin the conference. Be sure this is at the top of that file card. Otherwise, it might slip your mind.

(School Logo)

Dear Parents:

This next week begins a time for parent conferences at our school. You will be receiving a note from your child's teacher about the exact time and place of your conference later this week, but we would like to share with you some of the things that you might expect from us during this conference time and some of the things that we might expect from you.

As we work with your child, it is very important that you share information with us about your child's life at home. Here are some things that we might ask you during this conference time:

What does your child have to say about school at home?
What does your child enjoy doing at home?
What does your child spend most of his time doing at home?
Are there certain things that your child dreads doing?
What types of books or TV shows is your child most interested in?
How does your child get along with other members of the family? With friends at home?

There will also be some things that we will want to tell you about your child in school. Some of these might include:

how your child is progressing academically
how your child gets along with others in class and outside
what your child's special talents are here at school
sample tests and test scores
how your child seems to feel about himself/herself
the quality and quantity of work your child does

And there will be questions that you might want to ask us. If you can't think of any, we can offer a few as starters:

Does my child get the work done that should be done?
Does my child have good work habits?
How does my child respond to being told what to do?
How does my child respond when he makes a mistake?
Should I be expected to help with homework?
What can I do to help my child at home?

The conference will be a good time for both of us to learn about your child.

Sincerely,

OPEN HOUSE

Room Decorations
Be sure to post your class schedule on the board for the parents to see, and have your bulletin boards full of children's work attractively displayed. Frame the children's spelling words, have the children decorate the borders of their math papers, place papers in folders on the children's desks (folders that the children have decorated).

It's a Small World
From a large roll of butcher paper, cut out a set of paper dolls holding hands. If you want, cut them in groups which show the children's reading groups, rows the children sit in, or another grouping you choose.

Let each child ''dress'' one of the dolls to look like himself using material swatches, yarn, buttons, crayons, markers, etc. You may have to work in the hall. When the other teachers see you, they might join in. You can put the dolls up in the hallway.

Find Me, Find My Desk
Have children lie face down on pieces of paper and trace around their shapes. They can get into any position they want.

Let the children color in their shapes during free time for a week or longer. Provide other materials like those suggested in the activity above for those who wish to use them.

Place each child's portrait on his own desk the night of open house and ask the parents to locate their own child and sit in that desk for the start of your talks and demonstrations.

Clean Desks
Have the children clean the tops of their desks the day of open house by writing their spelling words on their desks with shaving cream. Choose a nice fragrance because the room will smell.

The insides of the desks can be cleaned in the same manner after the children carefully empty the desks of their contents.

Each school has a policy about having a function for introducing the parents to the school, classroom and their child's new teacher. All of us have been a part of many such functions as students and some of us as teachers. We suggest that you try some new ideas in addition to keeping the old ones that work best for you. Make sure that you meet parents, know their names, tell them about what their children will be studying, invite them to visit class, and tell them what is expected of their children in terms of behavior management.

Before School Open House
Open House is usually held during September. This is a good time because it gives parents a chance to meet their children's teachers early in the year. You might want to try having one before school starts. Try a daytime open house where parents and children can come to see the room, meet you, go through the textbooks, and meet other children and families informally.

Share-Our-Room Night
Have the parents and children arrive in the classroom at 7 p.m. and have a schedule of activities for them to take part in. Schedule each parent-child pair into 4-6 centers over the one-hour time slot. Rotate around the room yourself to talk with the pairs about the classroom activities. Let the children tell their parents about what they usually do in these subjects or centers.

Schedule 15-30 minutes to give the parents an overview of the total day of the children and your philosophy of education. Be sure that you provide time for questions.

What a View
Make a set of slides during the first month of school of the children in your classroom working. If you are more adept at working the video camera and recorder, videotape the children at work and play.

Have a continuous showing of these slides and tapes during the open house time.

Be Your Child
Have the children put their names on their desks. On each desk have an envelope with the parents' names on it and a letter from the child thanking them for coming and telling them about school as well as a letter from you thanking them for coming and giving them an outline of topics you will discuss during the evening. Have the parents become a child as you present lessons in various subject areas or motivating activities on a certain theme.

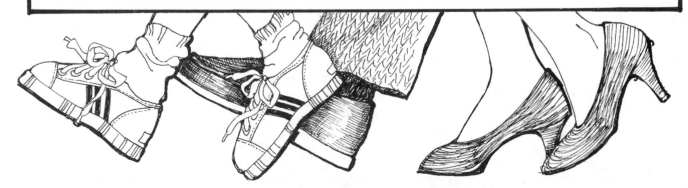

Make It and Leave It Night

As part of the open house evening at the school, have a room where parents can go to make games, centers, and other manipulatives for use in their child's classroom. Set it up with one "expert" to monitor, a set of instructions, materials and supplies, and possible assembly line guidelines. This is a good use for that extra room in your school (if you have one). A Parent Resource Room can be a place with parent reading materials as well as guidelines and supplies for making classroom learning games, posters, bulletin boards, etc.

This Is My Talent Night

Have individual or small groups of children share their "talents" at certain centers in the room.

Provide 4-6 centers or areas where children will tell parents about what they do and have done in the area or subject matter. Station 4-6 children at each area in order that they all simultaneously share their talents and interests with the parents.

Scavenger Hunt

The purpose of this activity is to have parents meet all of the adults that their children meet daily—the reading teacher, the math teacher, the homeroom teacher, the P.E. teacher, the resource room teacher, the building office staff, the principal, the librarian, the music teacher, the art teacher, etc.

Start the evening with a meeting of all parents and children in the gym for a greeting to the school and directions for the scavenger hunt. Provide parents with schedules of which rooms they should go to in which order. (Each homeroom teacher should be responsible for providing them for her parents.) Invitations to a reception should be developed and cut into pieces. One piece should be pasted on-to a piece of construction paper. At each room parents get another piece of their puzzle.

Each parents-child team goes on a search for a clue to solve a puzzle which is an invitation to the gym or library for refreshments after their travels are finished.

Demonstration Night

When new discipline strategies, reading programs, social studies curriculum, science materials, etc., are adopted by your system or school, have a special night where you invite your parents in to show them the new materials or techniques for understanding.

Encourage the parents to participate or ask questions about the new materials. Be sure to have on hand one of the selection committee at a neutral place where "heated" questions can be fielded away from the larger group.

Quiz Bowl

This activity is described more thoroughly in another section of this book (page 64).

During the school year a plastic fishbowl is filled with cards that have questions (with answers on the backs) for all curriculum areas. Each time something new is studied, new questions are placed in the bowl. At different times during the day, questions are drawn from the bowl and children answer them. The children use the bowl during center and free times.

At the beginning of the year, have a contest between the children and their parents as an introduction to what the children are studying. Challenge the parents to another quiz bowl at that time to be held at the end of the year. Perhaps the parents will ask their children more about what they are studying. Perhaps, though, the children might be willing to share less.

Let's Meet the Teacher

Have the parents sit in their children's chairs. At each child's desk have one question that you think parents might want to ask or have answered. Have each parent read the question and provide answers to the group.

Open the door for further questions at the end of the time.

Kids Can Answer Questions (to go along with above activity)

As the questions are devised by you, decide on groups of children to provide demonstrations to answer the questions for the parents. Be sure that each child has a part, and you can be relatively assured that all parents will attend.